YOU DON'T HAVE TO DRESS TO KILL

*Early female Shotokan karateka of the
British Isles (1957–1966)*

GW00370944

OTHER BOOKS BY CLIVE LAYTON

Conversations with Karate Masters
Unmasking the Martial Artist
Mysteries of the Martial Arts
Mind Training for the Martial Arts
Training with Funakoshi
Karate Master: The Life & Times of Mitsusuke Harada
Shotokan Dawn: Vol. I
Shotokan Dawn: Vol. II
A Shotokan Karate Book of Facts: Vol. I
A Shotokan Karate Book of Facts: Vol. II
A Shotokan Karate Book of Facts: Vol. III
The Kanazawa Years
Reminiscences by Master Mitsusuke Harada
A Shotokan Karate Book of Dates
The Shotokan Karate Book of Quotes
Kanazawa, 10th Dan
Funakoshi on Okinawa
Shotokan Dawn Over Ireland
The Shotokan Dawn Supplement
Shotokan Horizon

YOU DON'T HAVE TO DRESS TO KILL

Early female Shotokan karateka of the British Isles (1957–1966)

DR. CLIVE LAYTON

&

DR. DINUSHNI MUTHUCUMARANA

SAISHO PUBLICATIONS

PO Box 799, Harrow, GU1 9GT, England

First Published in 2007
by
SAISHO PUBLICATIONS
PO Box 799, Harrow, GU1 9GT, England
email: saishopub@hotmail.co.uk

First Edition

British Library Cataloguing-in-Publication Data.
A catalogue record for this book is available from the British Library.

ISBN 978 0 9555928 0 5

DEDICATIONS

Clive Layton:

TO

RACHEL, PANDORA & FRITHA

three very special souls

Dinushni Muthucumarana:

TO

MY PARENTS

to whom I owe everything

and to

KANISHKA

my husband, my best friend

ACKNOWLEDGEMENTS

The authors are grateful to the following people for their help during the preparation of this book: Rachel Layton; Pandora Layton; Vernon Bell, 10th Dan, Chief Instructor to Tenshin-Shinyo-Ryu Jujitsu (European Jujitsu Union), 3rd Dan Judo, 3rd Dan Karate-do; Alan Ruddock, 6th Dan Aikido, Butokukai; Pauline Bindra, 8th Dan, Chief Instructor to International Shotokan Karate; Nicholas Adamou, 8th Dan, Chief Instructor to the International Association of Shotokan Karate; Terence Wingrove, 9th Dan, International Ju Jitsu Federation, 7th Dan, Federation of All Japan Karate Organizations; Walter Seaton, 8th Dan, Chief Instructor to the England Karate-Do Wado-Kai; Gordon Thompson, 3rd Dan; Dorothy Naylor, 3rd Dan; Dr. Kanishka Samarasinghe, 3rd Dan.

Photo Credits: Clive Layton: 32, 50; Rachel Layton: 84; Dorothy Naylor: 69, 72; Saisho Publications: 14, 17, 23, 26, 27, 29, 31, 34-37, 41, 42, 45–47, 54–57, 59–62, 66, 68; Kanishka Samarasinghe: 85; Gordon Thompson: 63, 64.

Publisher's Appeal: The publisher of this work has been unable to trace or contact a number of owners (original photographer or other) of photographs used in this book. Such uncredited persons will be duly acknowledged by the publisher in any future edition of this book upon notification of proof of entitlement.

Front cover: Dorothy 'Dot' Naylor demonstrating with Frank Vernon at the Liverpool Red Triangle *dojo* (1966). Photo courtesy of the *Liverpool Daily Post* and *Echo*.

Back cover: Unknown female *karateka* demonstrating *yoko-geri-kekomi* on Frank Vernon at the Liverpool Red Triangle *dojo* (1966). Photo courtesy of the *Liverpool Daily Post* and *Echo*.

CONTENTS

PREFACE

The earliest karate organisation in Great Britain, the British Karate Federation, was founded by Vernon Bell, a professional judo instructor, on 1st April 1957. The story of karate's emergence and early history in Britain, from 1956 to 1966, tracing the Yoseikan (a *dojo* located in Shizuoka, Japan) based Shotokan to the Shotokan of the Japan Karate Association, has been recorded using the surviving records of the BKF as a backbone in Layton's two volume, *Shotokan Dawn*[1], *The Shotokan Dawn Supplement*[2], and, the yet to be published, *The Liverpool Red Triangle (1959-1966) & the Formation of the KUGB.*[3] Additionally, further important information is to be found in *Shotokan Dawn Over Ireland*[4], which charts early Shotokan in Eire (1960-1964).

The earliest female *karateka* in the British Isles were present, training and grading during the first ten years in question. BKF membership records exist for seventeen women and girls, while other BKF written and/or photographic evidence account for another three. Additionally, another four are mentioned as a result of interviewing, but their names, and whether they actually became members of the BKF, are unknown. For the years 1957 to 1966, the BKF archive shows one thousand two hundred and fourteen members, thus making a ratio of a little over 70:1, male to female, or to put it another way, 1.4 per cent of BKF members for whom membership forms have survived for the period under investigation, were female. Also, of the thirty BKF clubs throughout those first ten years, only eight had female licence holders and two seem to have had females training for a very brief period without licences ever having been taken out. This book, then, concentrates upon a most unusual group of individuals, not only within the early BKF, but also in society at large, whose values and expectations for females, though changing, were somewhat more delineated and rigid than they are today.

Clearly, this work is concerned with a period before decimalization took place in Great Britain and in order to keep a sense of the spirit of the time, the authors have retained the old systems. For readers too young to remember, for length, there were twelve inches in one foot and three feet in one yard. An inch is 25.4 millimetres, a foot is 0.305 of a metre and a yard is 0.914 of a metre. In terms of weight, there were sixteen ounces in a pound and fourteen pounds in a stone. An ounce is 28.35 grams, a pound is 0.453 of a kilogram, and a stone is 6.35 kilograms. However, by far the most frequent calculation the reader will be required to make, should he or she so desire, is the conversion of money. The pre-decimalization system employed the rule that there were twelve pennies in a shilling (six pennies in sixpence, of course), and twenty shillings in a pound. Half a crown equalled two shillings and sixpence. For conversion purposes, a shilling equals 5p, therefore £1 8s. equals £1.40; £1. 8s 6d equals £1.43 (rounded up as there are no longer halfpence). If the new values had been placed in brackets after the old values in the text, which would have been a straightforward procedure, the flow of the book, at times, would have been spoilt, and would repeatedly have taken the reader away from the past to the present, and this the authors did not wish.

The limited number of Japanese words, bar two, with the exception of proper nouns, have been italicised for easy reference. The two exceptions to this rule are 'dan' and 'kyu.' 'Dan' is to be found in most concise English dictionaries and refers to black belt rank – the higher the dan, the higher the rank. 'Kyu' (non black belt rank) is not italicised because it is met with fairly frequently and contrasts with dan. Unlike dan rank, the lower, numerically, the kyu grade, the higher the holder's proficiency. A short glossary of karate terms is provided on page 81.

If there are errors in the present work, though great care has been taken to minimise such errors, then the authors would like to apologise in advance. It has only been possible to work with the material that has survived, or that the authors have been privy to, and any errors are made in good faith. Errors detected to date are almost exclusively related to Bell's handwriting, which can be extremely difficult to read. Also, once again, and with Bell's previous permission, it was felt that his desire for overly long sentences at times had to be corrected to aid reader comfort; similarly, incorrect grammar has, occasionally, been addressed.

A rough estimate suggests that something in the region of one in four *karateka* training in Britain today is female. This, then, reflects a marked change over the last forty to fifty years. This is, no doubt, partly as a result of changes in society and personal perception, but also, one feels, reflects a change in training. The British Isles, when the young, and not so young ladies featured in this short book donned their *gis*, was certainly a different place. The purpose here has been to record all the available information, so that these pioneers of women's karate, even though most may have trained only briefly, are not forgotten.

The humorous, somewhat tongue-in-cheek title of this work, although still a popular saying today, was suggested by reading a woman reporter's account, writing about women's self-defence, in 1966. It has thus been retained to impart a spirit of the time. The sub-title, though more formal, actually reveals the book's contents, of course.

March, 2007

CLIVE LAYTON, M.A., Ph.D (Lond), C. Psychol., CSci., AFBPsS., 7th Dan.

DINUSHNI MUTHUCUMARANA, M.B., B.S. (Lond), FRCOphth., 1st Dan.

YOU DON'T HAVE TO DRESS TO KILL

Vernon Bell, the founder of the British karate movement, arranged with Henri Plee, the dominant figure in the emergence of European karate, for a visit from one of his senior students, the diminutive Vietnamese, Hoang Nam, of the Fédération Francaise de Karaté, to give a two hour karate course on the tennis court of Bell's parents' home at 12, Maybush Road, Hornchurch, Essex, on Sunday, 21st July 1957. Nam's course was followed by a visit from an ITN news crew, which led to the first karate film ever broadcast on national television (on the evening of 22nd July 1957) in Great Britain. Considering Bell had only formed the BKF on 1st April that year, we are most fortunate that his enthusiasm to promote the art has left us with such an invaluable, early archival source.

In a letter to Plee dated the 26th July 1957, Bell noted that twelve pupils attended the course. Names of eleven males are known: D. Blake, P. Brandon, B. Dolan, D. Dyer, Ken Elliott, Trevor Guilfoyle, Michael Manning, Brian Miles, L. Pearson, James Trotter and Gerald Tucker. These students appeared in the black and white film (and five of them featured in photographs of the first karate demonstration ever given by members of the BKF at Melbourne Fields, Valentines Park, Ilford, on the 20th July). The question arises as to who the twelfth pupil was.

Following the filming, Nam held a grading and nine men passed. In Bell's own words, the following then happened: 'After the grading, I took the class on tactics and movement whilst Mr. Nam gave one hour's private instruction to our only lady pupil, Miss Higgins, in which Mr. Nam taught her his new ladies' *kata* for the first time, and after the lesson Mr. Nam graded her 6th kyu as he thought she had progressed very well' (letter to Plee, 26th July 1957).[5] On the basis of this evidence, Higgins has the distinction of being the first woman not only to have trained in karate in Great Britain, but to be graded also.

Vernon Bell, founder of the British karate movement, encouraged women students to train in karate from the outset.

Whether Higgins actually took a complete and standard BKF grading, in that it was the same as for her male contemporaries, is unknown, though her grading went unrecorded in the BFK Grading Register. The grading results were not entered in the register by Bell until the 16th September 1957, so perhaps Higgins had stopped training and her name was omitted on that basis?

Bell was almost certainly referring to Higgins again in his 26th July letter, when he wrote of the evening of Monday, 22nd July, that Nam 'took his last class of six pupils and one lady and this concluded a very instructive and pleasant weekend for all of us.'[6] Bell's language is, perhaps, suggestive of some form of lesson segregation based on sex. However, assuming he was referring to Higgins, he had already noted that she was a 'pupil,' so, it seems likely that Bell wished to draw to Plee's attention, once again, the fact that the infant BKF not only welcomed female students, but actually had one, otherwise he could simply have written 'seven pupils.'

No BKF membership form has survived for Higgins, and one wonders whether she actually ever completed one. Whilst BKF records have regrettably not survived for a few of these early members, the possible loss of Higgins's membership form is, on balance, unlikely. Apart from the fact that she was unmarried, her identity, and what became of her, are tantalising mysteries. Unfortunately, Higgins is a common surname and it is a great shame that her first name is not known, otherwise some detective work could have been undertaken. Thirty-eight years later, Bell was asked what he could recall about her and the authors regret to report that he 'had no recollections of a Miss Higgins at all.'[7] A further eight years on, however, he was asked the same question, to which the reply was that she had 'black, curly, floppy hair.'[8] Perhaps something had jolted his memory in the intervening period? Then again, maybe he made a simple mistake, for whilst the next woman to be featured did not have black hair, it was certainly curly and floppy, and the two women appear to have trained remarkably close in time.

Whether Higgins was the twelfth student is unknown. There was one other possible male trainee known to the authors for whom a record survives, who could have attended the course, a certain R. Armsby, but the question is raised as to why he was not shown on the film. Certainly, Bell's 'twelve pupils' are referred to in an extremely early newspaper report[9] of the 21st June 1957, entitled, 'He is Bringing 'Killer' Sport to Britain,' by John Greenhalgh. In the very next sentence but one, the article continues, 'ages of the men Vernon Bell coaches,' so the language tends to sway towards twelve men. However, this was quite obviously a month before Nam's arrival, so one student could have dropped out and Higgins taken his place.

Two copies exist of a letter, dated the 20th June and 22nd June 1957, which is addressed to 'The Editor' of a number of newspapers, of which the above, and those below, are no doubt responses, introducing them to the BKF. The relevant passage here being: 'In the last few months I have been privileged to have in training under me about ten keen practising students of karate, of whom several have in this week been graded to their first grade in karate – that of white belt. These men, besides myself, are the first ever to achieve a grade in this country in the deadly and dangerous karate, and as these students of mine are all local and Essex men, I feel it is a distinction and an honour for them to be the pioneers of a new and highly skilled art in England.' So there is no mention of a woman from, effectively, the outset.

On 5th July 1957, another article in an unknown newspaper by an unknown writer, entitled 'Forbidden Sport Taught Here: Japanese

Fights Often Ended in Death,' the first sentence notes, 'a dozen young men.' Neither article excludes the possibility of a woman training – they just fail to mention one at all. If there had been a BKF woman student, it seems not that unlikely that she would have been mentioned, for Bell, keen to promote karate, could have made capital from it. On the other hand, he may not have wanted it generally known that a woman was training, for he was unsure how the public would react to the introduction of the 'killer sport' to men, let alone the fairer sex. He may have deemed it too much, too soon, and was simply being prudent.

In another early newspaper report of the 10th October 1957, in, *Reveille*, entitled, 'Secret 'Sportsmen' Train to Kill,' by Des Marwood, the opening words to the piece are, 'twelve men' and the title of the report tends to give it away in any case. A female student is not mentioned in this article either, though it was published several months after Nam's course.[10] However, Higgins could have left and her place taken up by another, male student.

It seems reasonable to assume that Higgins was there at the filming, even if she was not the twelfth student, but why she wasn't featured in the film is yet another mystery that is likely never to be solved, though it may well have been for the same reason she wasn't featured in newspaper articles.

Another extremely early female BKF student was Doris Keane. She, too, appears to have trained in 1957 and was photographed with P. Brandon, A. Dyer, J. Trotter and Bell in the garden of 12, Maybush Road. There is no evidence that Dyer and Brandon trained into 1958 and the trees in the garden in the said photograph are in full leaf, and Keane is in short sleeves, so the picture is almost certainly to have been taken in the summer of 1957. Yet there is some confusion, for Bell noted that 'in 1958 we had our very first female *karateka*, the very first woman to train in Great Britain. Her name was Doris Keane, from Romford. She trained for a few months at the St. Mary's *dojo*, but it was too much for her, too hard.'[11] Bell did not commence teaching karate at the British Legion Hall, St. Mary's Lane, Upminster, until January 1958. There is no mention of Keane in any literature of the time, especially when Bell was writing to Plee about the formation of the St. Mary's *dojo* and the students who enrolled on his first course. It must be said that in both conversation and in the written word, Bell was not always accurate with dates or locations.

Perhaps Keane was featured in the 1957 photograph having just practised judo, though she is not wearing a *gi*. The authors have no

Doris Keane (centre) with James Trotter and Vernon Bell to her left, respectively, and A. Dyer and P. Brandon to her right, respectively.

record of Brandon and Dyer ever having practised judo with Bell, though they probably did. They are wearing judo *gi*, but then karate *gi* were not readily available at the time. Trotter is beside Keane wearing a judo coloured belt, and we can deduce this because he does not appear in the BKF Grading Register until 1959. Dyer and Brandon were long departed by then, yet we know, through the film, that Trotter was there in 1957. But the point that probably best dates the photograph is Bell, for he is not only wearing a white *gi* – something he largely disregarded for karate practice in 1958, when he advocated BKF *karateka* wear black *gi* to differentiate them from *judoka* – but that he is wearing his Yoseikan karate black belt, with its alternating horizontal rectangles of black and red.

The occasion is unlikely to have been at the beginning/end of a ju-jitsu lesson either, for Bell never mentioned these students ever practised with him.

There are two other possibilities that need to be considered with regard to Keane. Her existence is known only through Bell, who readily identified her in the single photograph in which she is to be seen. But is the image really Keane? Perhaps this is Higgins – the date fits – and a photograph of Keane does not exist. However, Bell was very good at identifying faces in photographs and he never detracted from his opinion that the image was of Keane, so the authors have gone with that. There may be other reasons too, as to why he should have remembered her.

Bell recalled Keane, noting to Layton that she 'was keen.' Bell considered that she was 'about seventeen years old at the time' – and, as a matter of interest, remembered that she worked in an office and baby-sat – so the authors consulted the Birth Registers of the General Registration Office. Dates from January 1936 to December 1943 were searched, so the age span investigated, to allow for error on Bell's part, was, thirteen and a half to twenty-one, at the end of 1957. There was no record of a Doris Keane, or, in case of incorrect spelling (though Bell insisted the spelling was correct), a 'Doris Kean.' However, whilst there is no evidence to suggest that she was born in Romford, there were Keane births in the Romford registration district during that time, namely to women with the maiden names of Kelly, Daly and Wells. What was intriguing though, was that there was a certain Donis Keane born in the West Ham registration district (Vol. 4a, p. 90. Sept. 1942). The authors are unaware of Donis as a first name, and so this could well have been Doris, but then again, it could be Denis (though this is a variant spelling in the English-speaking world for 'Dennis.' Ironically, there is reference, later in this book, to an Irish *judoka* with the first name of 'Denis'). West Ham is only some eight miles, as the crow flies, from Romford, and when one considers that the GRO covers all of England, the coincidence of finding someone of that name so close to home base is fairly unlikely, not to say remote. If Doris Keane was born in July, August or September 1942 (GRO registers record the last of three months of registration {though she could have been born late in June – there sometimes being a cross-over period due to time given by the relevant party to register}), then she was likely to be nearly, or just fifteen years of age. The problem is that the woman in the photograph looks older, more like twenty.

If Keane was only fifteen, then Bell's contention that, 'we only took adults over eighteen, and initially only males,'[12] seems exceptionally short-lived. But then, Keane, like Higgins, although allowed to train, may never have actually been BKF members.

The authors were obviously obliged to obtain the Donis Keane certificate to determine, once and for all, whether this was 'their' Keane, and have to report that Donis was a transcription error in the Index for 'Denis.' This necessitated an extended search, and so the years 1930 to 1935 were taken into account, so the total span investigated would have made Doris Keane somewhere between about thirteen and a half and twenty-seven years of age. Whilst there were other Keanes to be found in Romford and West Ham, there was no Doris. However, there was a Doris P. Keane born in the last quarter of 1931 in the registration district of West Derby (Vol. 8b, p. 586) to a mother with the maiden name of Dumper. Whether this is our Doris Keane is unknown. If it is, then she was twenty-five years of age in the summer of 1957.

Working on the assumption that Bell could have recalled the spelling incorrectly, the authors, despite his insistence, looked at both Keen and Keene for the years October 1937 to December 1940. There were births of both spellings in the Romford registration district, but no Doris. However, there was a Doris Keen born in the first quarter of 1939 to a woman with the maiden name of Patterson, living in Liverpool (Vol. 8b, page 308). The age fits Bell's 'about seventeen' recollection, for she would have been eighteen at the time, but Bell never mentioned that she spoke with a Liverpool accent (though she could, of course, have moved when a child).

Bell, taking his responsibility of the introduction of karate to Britain seriously, was determined that new students wishing to train under the BKF must undergo a drawn out application procedure. They were obliged to supply two references, a medical certificate to show they were fit to train, had to complete an application form and an oath of allegiance form (both of which had to be endorsed), come forward before a committee to be vetted, pay dues to become a member and pay training fees in advance. This method was adhered to until 1965, when a simpler application procedure was introduced.

The authors are unaware of any male student being allowed to train under the BKF with Bell's knowledge, without first becoming a member. Bell was rigorous on this point. So, Higgins and Keane seemed to have been singled out and honoured, assuming they did not complete application forms, on the basis of their sex. What gave rise to this phenomenon is a mystery, though the authors have their suspicions.

The second possibility is that Higgins and Keane may be one of the same. In, *Shotokan Dawn Vol: I*, it was noted that 'it is remotely possible that Higgins was Keane's maiden name. The author says 'remotely' because it is most likely that Bell would have known if she was married.'[13] However, if Higgins was a 'Miss' and Keane only fifteen to 'about seventeen' years of age at the time, then she must have married at a very early age. Nevertheless, the authors checked the GRO Index of Marriages from July 1957 to December 1959, for Keane in England, to determine if any married a Higgins, and now report that none were to be found. The authors have not considered that Higgins may have changed her name by deed poll.

The karate that both Higgins and Keane would have learned was not what might readily be described today as that practised by the Japan Karate Association. Rather, it was the karate of the famous Yoseikan that had been introduced to France chiefly by Jean Alcheik (in the early 1950s) and Hiroo Mochizuki (in 1956) through the offices of Plee. It is unknown whether Mochizuki had trained at the JKA at this time, but photographs from 1957 reveal a style and *kata* highly reminiscent of more recent Shotokan, yet with touches of an older Shotokan. However, his famous father, Minoru Mochizuki, a *judoka* and *aikidoka* of note, and Chief Instructor to the Yoseikan, had trained with Gichin Funakoshi (the founder of Shotokan and the Okinawan credited with introducing karate to Japan) in the 1930s, though this would have been what might be best described as an 'older version' of the style, yet still readily recognizable. It wouldn't be until August 1958 that Bell would come under the influence of a known JKA trained black belt grade, in the form of Tetsuji Murakami, and it wouldn't be until July 1959 that Murakami would visit England.[14]

Although there is no solid evidence for a woman training in BKF karate through 1958 until towards the end of 1961, Bell was not averse to trying to secure female members. A good example of this was to be seen in the literature of the 1st BKF Summer School held at the Imperial Private Hotel, 9-11 Ramshill Drive, South Cliff, Scarborough, Yorkshire, from the 7th–12th September 1959. The course details reveal that the training was open to, 'either sex over sixteen and under fifty-five years of age.' Whilst an amusing aside is to be noted on the single, foolscap page details, in that it revealed that the course was under the direction of Mrs. C. F. Bell (and yes, there *was* a typing error, and also an omission, for Bell's initials were 'V.C.F.' {Vernon Cecil Frederick}), the course did not attract a female student.

The following year, the poster for the 2nd BKF Annual Summer Course, held between the 14th–26th August 1960, at the same location, noted that the course was 'open to any person, either sex, over fifteen years.' Course details, however, reveal no dropping of the minimal age, in that, 'any person, either male or female, over the age of sixteen years, whether with or without any knowledge of karate may enrol on the course.' The details continued: 'No experience or special ability in any other sport is necessary to be able to learn karate, which is a completely different and unusual form of sport unlike any other, and any average person of normal intelligence, [and] reasonable physical fitness can benefit from its training. It is easy to learn [and] it requires no special aptitude or ability. Karate is of special benefit to women because it is graceful, smooth and agile, and has harmonious movements. There is no risk of injury whatsoever if one practises seriously. Age is of no account in becoming efficient in this art, neither is size or weight. It is the finest form of self-defence known, as well as being one of the finest systems of physical culture, moral training and self-discipline, … [which] most other sports lack. It is said that once you have tried karate, all other sports are tame in comparison and you never leave it.' This description was evident in subsequent course literature.

The possible dropping of the minimum age and the assurance that karate training was beneficial to women appeared to fall on deaf ears, for no woman was to enrol on this course either.

However, the following year, more than four years after the founding of the BKF and the brief training span of Higgins and Keane, a woman did 'rise to the bait' after witnessing a BKF summer school, and she has the distinction of being the first woman for whom records survive to complete an application for BKF membership.

Suzette Pauline Hubbard wrote to the BKF somewhere between the 7th and 17th August 1961, and details were sent back to her on the 17th of that month. The BKF Register of Enquiries records four hundred and twenty-two entries to February 1964, and Hubbard was listed as Nō. 146. She signed her completed form on the 31st September 1961, though the accompanying Private and Class Declaration and Oath of Allegiance form was signed more than one month before, on the 22nd August – this discrepancy being something of a mystery. At the time, she was forty-three years of age, having been born on the 16th June 1918, and was living in Clacton-on-Sea, Essex. She was married and gave her occupation as 'guest house proprietor.' She had seen service in Air Raid Patrol throughout World War II, and then, again, in the Merchant Navy during 1956-1957. She reported being in good health and listed nursing (being a First Aid Superintendent) a hobby, as well as having many varied interests. She also enjoyed swimming and playing table tennis. She was a member of the Clacton Judo Club based at the Station Hotel, Clacton, and had reached the rank of yellow belt on the 11th June 1961, under Eric Dominy. She had heard of the BKF through her judo club, but was introduced through Tetsuji Murakami, having seen karate performed at Seawick. She wished to learn karate for exercise and as a 'further means of defence not covered by judo movement,' and noted that karate had 'movements more graceful for women' – her choice of words, perhaps, reflecting the course literature that she had, no doubt, been given. She planned to train once a week from October to March – presumably the quiet period for business. The last date, in Bell's handwriting, which appears on the bottom of her application form is 7th January 1963, and seems to involve payment of some kind.

Hubbard's referee, a Dr. J. Manuel, of Holland-on-Sea, Essex, noted on the 22nd August that she was 'of good character and a responsible person,' whilst her second referee (from a signature that looks like W. Lunn, of the Osborne Hotel, Clacton-on-Sea,) wrote on the 14th August 1961, that he had 'always found her to be a most conscientious and trustworthy person, of sober habits, and a morally fit person to be instructed in the art of karate.'

Hubbard mentioned seeing karate at Seawick and having been introduced to the art by Murakami. The authors have been unable to locate a Seawick, though this almost certainly refers to an ancient hamlet dating back beyond the Norman Conquest. Hubbard was actually introduced to karate at Seaview Holiday Lido, some two miles from the village of St. Osyth, along Beach Road, a third-class concrete road, where she witnessed the BKF Summer School held under Murakami from the 5th–12th August, that year. Hubbard would have watched Murakami and his students training on the highly polished Marley-tiled floor, under the coloured lighting of the Entertainments Pavilion, based at the centre of the holiday camp. The week-long course was to be of major significance in the history of Shotokan in the British Isles, most notably for the students who attended. Edward Ainsworth and Alan Ruddock, who introduced Shotokan karate, if not karate itself, to Scotland and Ireland, respectively, were there, as were Gordon Thompson and Douglas Pettman, who started early provincial BKF *dojos* in York and Lincoln, respectively. Details of this course are given elsewhere.[15]

Hubbard never appears to have graded, and, indeed, it is unknown for sure where she trained, assuming she did, nor for how many times, but it is believed, almost certainly, that it was at the St. Mary's *dojo*, being the closest BKF club to her, though involving a return trip of more than one hundred miles. It is possible that she could have caught the train from Clacton to London and trained at the London *dojo*, which was based, at the time, in an upstairs room above the Horseshoe public house, 24, Clerkenwell Close, London, EC1. Bell referred to Hubbard as 'one of the earliest, original lady members,' but could remember absolutely nothing about her, and, regrettably, no photograph has survived.

The woman standing extreme right is unknown – RAF Scampton (1961/62)

Bell plugged away at karate demonstrations for many years, both indoor and outdoor, trying to attract students of either sex. On Tuesday, 28th February 1961, for example, a demonstration was given to the Hornchurch Division of the Young Conservatives. A letter from a Miss A. Kerr, the Honorary Secretary, makes it clear the display of judo and Japanese boxing (karate) went very well. She noted, 'I think most of the members realised the advantage of knowing a few of the more simple throws and it was great fun being given the opportunity to actually try some on your patient and willing pupils.' Of course, Kerr is probably referring to audience participation in judo, though there are throws in karate too.

An intriguing group photograph exists showing members of the BKF *dojo* at RAF Scampton, Lincolnshire. Besides and slightly behind the instructor, the aforementioned Douglas Pettman, stands a woman in a white judo *gi*. Her name is unknown and, like Higgins and Keane, she almost certainly did not become a member of the BKF. The Scampton *dojo* was established on the 20th September 1961, though it appears that BKF affiliation was short-lived. Little is known about this *dojo*, though thirteen BKF membership application forms, all male, have survived. Bell conducted two gradings at the club, the last being on the 14th February 1962. It is possible, though unlikely, that the unidentified woman's surname was Aston, Dudley, Farrell, Gibbons, Green, or Knight. As she is not referred to directly in any surviving

23

correspondence between Pettman and Bell, it is possible that she was a friend of Bell's who had travelled from London with him, for a woman of sorts is referred to in correspondence, and it appears to have caused Bell problems with his host's wife, who had access to a now lost letter that Bell wanted destroyed. Yet it remains unclear as to whether Bell actually brought a woman to Lincoln or not. Terry Wingrove, however, one of the BKF's senior students, having joined in 1959, and who became a BKF instructor of note, wrote: 'I do not think she was a girlfriend of Vernon's, as he kept them close to home (London area).'[16] Wingrove also recalled: 'I only went to Scampton once and the woman [in the photograph] obviously did not make any impression on me' [as he couldn't recall her].[16] Nevertheless, there she is standing, wearing a *gi* in a group karate photograph, so she is likely to have trained, albeit maybe only once or twice, though her presence is sufficient for inclusion in this book.

Film and television, perhaps, played a role in bringing women to the karate *dojo*. In Britain, Honor Blackman, from 1962, in the immensely popular, *The Avengers*, co-starring ex-Etonian Patrick Macnee, was the escape for the imaginative woman and, possibly, female *karateka* to be. Blackman seemed to combine judo with touches of karate in her weekly portrayal as Cathy Gale. Her character was a first for British television. Sexually alluring, intelligent, refined, dressed in a leather utility suit and the infamous boots, she added a strange, almost bizarre element to the series that later was reflected in decidedly surreal episodes. Blackman gave up this lucrative and influential role to play Pussy Galore in a 1964 film that probably had more influence than any other at that time in bringing martial arts to a wide western audience – the third, and probably best James Bond movie, United Artists' *Goldfinger*, directed by Guy Hamilton. The film was made in England and grossed nearly twenty million dollars in one year, making it one of the all-time money-making movies, and allowed Sean Connery (playing Bond) to enter the Annual Top Ten Box Office Stars' list.

Whilst Blackman, sure enough, had a judo encounter with Connery, it was Goldfinger's seemingly invincible bodyguard, Oddjob, played by Harold Sakata, with his razor-edged bowler hat, that, for many, men especially, one imagines, stole the show. Whereas Bond was obviously 'high-class' comic strip, there was something undeniably powerful and permanent about the inscrutable Oddjob.

Blackman was replaced in *The Avengers* by Diana Rigg, who, dressed in a PVC catsuit, played Emma Peel. Rigg appeared no less impressive on the martial arts front, incorporating more karate techniques.

The best of the Blackman/Rigg episodes regarding karate is *The Cybernauts* (first broadcast on the 16th October 1965), where Steed and Peel investigate a series of broken necks from devastating blows. Peel is obliged to infiltrate a karate club in order to solve the mystery and fights a woman black belt in the process.

The whole image of the martial arts continued to grow more popular through this unusual series. Men and women alike were impressed by the way Blackman and Rigg disposed of villains. It may have been way-out fiction, but it was new and entertaining, and people liked it. Rigg, of course, was chosen to play the ill-fated wife of Bond in the film, *On Her Majesty's Secret Service*, in 1969.

Bell never realised his ambition of having a book on karate published, despite considerable effort. *The Manual of Karate-Do* was completed around 1963 and would have been 'The official handbook of the British Karate Federation.' As far as can be deduced, Bell had planned as part of the final, twelfth, section of the book, surprisingly detailed information on how to become a member of the BKF. The very first paragraph of this inclusion noted that: 'All categories of membership are open to any man or woman between the ages of 16 – 60, irrespective of nationality.' It appears, then, that Bell still wished to operate a minimum age of sixteen, but had increased the maximum age for commencement by an additional five years.

Alan Ruddock, already referred to, had a BKF branch up and running in Dublin and in a letter to Bell dated the 6th August 1963, we get our first mention of intending female students. Ruddock wrote: 'We have had requests from two girls regards joining (one is a judo blue belt) ... We can quite easily arrange another class for women on Saturday (giving us three ordinary classes and one women's). I write on this point mainly to ask you if there is any modification in techniques as taught to women. If all is okay, I will forward these girls' applications to you as soon as they are ready.' Three days later, in another letter to Bell, Ruddock again refers to the 'girls' forms.'

The two girls who joined were, almost certainly, Bernadette Berigan and Carmel Byrne. These two young ladies hold the distinction of being, surely, the first to practise Shotokan in Ireland, if not karate, irrespective of style.

Berigan, who was born on the 4th April 1944, was thus nineteen when she signed her BKF application for membership form on the 8th August 1963. The membership fee was ten shillings. A machinist by

Alan Ruddock, instructor to the BKF Dublin *dojo*, who encouraged women students to train.

occupation, she gave her sole hobby/interest as judo, of which she was indeed the blue-belt referred to, and she trained at the Irish Judo Association, based at 32, Parkgate Street, Dublin. Denis Conniffe, honorary secretary to the Irish Judo Association, acted as a referee. He wrote that she 'has been an outstanding member of this club for some years. She is of impeccable character and honesty and has assisted the club in many ways, for example, by taking part in judo shows and demonstrations. I am sure she will prove a worthy member of any other club she joins.' Her second referee (whose signature cannot be read) of the City Quay Presbytery, noted that she came 'from a very good-living family. She is careful about the performance of her religious duties. I can recommend her as being honest, trustworthy and of good character.' Berigan declared that she was able to train in karate some three times per week.

Byrne was born on the 28th December 1946, and was thus sixteen at the time of signing her BKF application for membership form on the 24th September 1963 (though the Oath of Allegiance was signed on the 5th October). A shop assistant by occupation, she, too, was a member of the IJA (listing judo as her only hobby/interest) and

 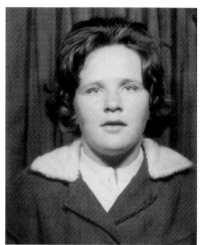

Bernadette Berigan (1963)   Carmel Byrne (1963)

Conniffe, acting as a referee once more, wrote that she was 'an able and trusted member of the club. I, and every other club member, can vouch for her integrity and reliability. I am confident she will reflect credit on every club and organisation she may join.' A former employer (a newsagents and tobacconists) also described her as 'an honest and industrious worker ... [who could be] highly recommended to any position of trust.'

To January 1964, there is no BKF evidence that either Berigan or Byrne graded. This is hardly surprising however, as they would have been training only a few months before the Dublin branch resigned from the BKF to register with the JKA directly. Certainly, at least to the end of 1963, they would have trained at the CIE Hall, Inchicore, Dublin. A letter by John Robinson (who took over from Ruddock at the Dublin *dojo* when Ruddock went to sea) to Bell on the 11th May 1964, noted thirty-four members at the club. It is not known for certain whether Berigan and Byrne were included in these, though thirty-four Dublin BKF membership forms have survived, so it seems likely that they were. No BKF photographs are in existence, at least to the authors' knowledge, of these two women in karate *gi*, and for their images, we are entirely dependent on the passport-size photographs they submitted with their BKF applications. As far as the authors are aware, members of the Dublin club remained ungraded throughout 1964 (by which time Murakami was deemed out of favour) for no officially recognised official JKA instructor was in Europe to grade them. From May 1965 to May 1966, Hirokazu Kanazawa resided in London and travelled throughout Great Britain for the BKF, but there is no record of him travelling to Eire during that time.[17] At the end of 1965, Keinosuke Enoeda took up residence in Liverpool, but the authors do not know whether he travelled to Dublin.

Despite Bell's apparent attempts to secure female students, the 'committee acceptance form' wording (readers will be reminded that perspective BKF students had to submit themselves before a committee and be interviewed, before Bell would consider their application) does not allow for them, so: 'The under mentioned person has today been brought before this committee, *his* particulars thoroughly investigated, and it is the decision of this committee that we approve and recommend that *he* be granted approval by the central committee for membership of the British Karate Federation' (authors' italics). A year on, 1964, the wording remained unchanged. Rather than any deliberate act on Bell's part, the form's wording was likely to have been a subconscious acceptance that attracting potential women students was extremely unlikely.

Whereas Hubbard, the reader may recall, was the first record of a woman in the BKF Register of Enquiries, the second and last entry for females (as far as it is possible to tell) came in late October, early November, 1963, when Christine Alexander, who was residing, temporarily, at an address in South Woodford, Essex, requested information, quoting *Zen Combat* (as did others) as her inspiration for writing. Full details were duly sent back to her on the 14th November. She is recorded as No. 380 in the said register. She did not join the BKF and nothing else is known of her. The authors are unaware as to what, exactly, the medium *Zen Combat* took.

Of the twenty-eight women assumed or known to have trained in Shotokan, however briefly, with the BKF to the summer of 1966, five, the greatest number from any one BKF *dojo*, came from the N.E. Yorkshire and S. Durham BKF Branch, better known as the Middlesbrough club, run by Fred Kidd and Walter Seaton. One exceptional young lady who began training at the *dojo*, Pauline Laville (later to become Pauline Fuller; now Pauline Bindra), stood out way above all other female BKF *karateka* at the time, to become not only the first female JKA black-belt in Britain, but, more than forty years on, to hold the rank of 8th Dan and to head her own karate association – International Shotokan Karate. It is not known exactly when Bindra started karate training at Middlesbrough, for it appears that Bell destroyed her original application form, assuming one existed, when

Fred Kidd and Walter Seaton, instructors of the BKF Middlesbrough *dojo*, who encouraged women students to train in karate.

she moved to London and joined the Horseshoe pub *dojo* in Clerkenwell, when she was obliged to complete a new one. For what it is worth, Bindra was ungraded in March 1964. She had been training in judo for four years at the prestigious Middlesbrough Judo Club founded by Kidd and Syd Carr (and four unknown others), which had some two hundred and fifty members (being one of the largest clubs in England) at that time, of which a quarter were women, and she had reached the rank of blue belt. She had been advised against taking an interest in karate.

Bindra recalled: 'When I first studied judo and karate, I never told my parents because they wouldn't have let me go … my sister paid for my karate lessons and judo lessons because I had no money and she was working. It was only after a while I told my parents.[18]

'The judo instructors kept saying this [karate] is really bad stuff, you shouldn't do it, it's just started in this country, it's evil, and all this rubbish. So, we [Bindra and a few friends] went down there to have a go at Walter [for sending them letters about karate practice] and we saw it and we liked it.'[19] 'The [Middlesbrough] *dojo* was just down the road from where I lived; within walking distance.'[18]

Bindra used to train at the *dojo*, which she recalled had a very dark wooden floor which often gave rise to splinters in the feet, 'two or three nights a week. I only ever saw about six people [at a lesson]. There were three girls, but they dropped out ... I remember going up and down in these funny stances, and thinking what the hell am I doing this for? Walter Seaton was such a kind, considerate instructor. So calm, so much patience. I couldn't believe that anybody would have such patience with us stupid women ... I think we all have Walter Seaton to thank for bringing women into karate as early as he did, because if he hadn't had the foresight to do it, nobody would have bothered ... I remember there were punch-bags hanging up and men hitting them. I thought, 'I'll never be able to hit like that.' I said, 'How do you expect me to do that?' and Walter said, 'Don't worry, you don't have to do it.' Walter Seaton was a brown-belt, and Fred Kidd was a brown-belt. I was totally confused, but I liked it.'[19]

'With judo I was at a disadvantage because of my [small] size, but with karate I didn't see a disadvantage ... there weren't any weight divisions [in judo] in those days ... [and] I'd get smashed down on my head.'[18]

Seaton recalled: 'I do remember very well Pauline starting training. She joined our club, the Budokan, in Middlesbrough, along with a group of girls who were all nurses at the Middlesbrough General Hospital.

'In the late 1950s to mid 1960s, karate was a very hard fighting art and like boxing it was considered to be a male fighting art, which included self-defence. When Pauline started training, her membership of our club and karate practice was simply considered for self-defence. However, within just a few weeks, Pauline gave me a shock and proved my basic belief that karate was a male fighting art was totally incorrect and that she was going to be a first-class *karateka*.

'One picture that has never left my mind was Pauline's front-kicks; they were so technically correct – they were a perfect example of how front-kicks should be performed ... [demonstrating] full speed and power. In addition to her good techniques came an outstanding, and I mean outstanding, display of fighting spirit.'[20]

The fact that Bindra recalled that she started training with three other women, and this is backed up by Seaton noting 'a group of girls,' obviously suggests other female *karateka* training in BKF karate of which nothing else is known.

At the end of 1963, Bindra travelled south with her sister, Louise, in the hope of finding work. They lived at a hostel, Warwickshire House, in Gower Street, London, WC1. In Middlesbrough, Pauline had indeed been a trainee nurse, 'But I didn't like it ... they didn't give me time off to do karate,'[19] she recalled. 'Luckily I learned typing at school. It was where you got your fingers rapped with a ruler if you looked at the keys. So I passed my RSA exams at school, and I got a

Pauline Bindra (née Laville) (1964)

typing job in London. The wages were fantastic compared to what they were in the north of England.'[19]

Bindra continued: 'Walter had given me the address where to go to train ... I said to him, 'Are there any women there?' and he said, 'No. You won't find any women [training in karate] anywhere.

'I remember the first time I went to Vernon Bell's *dojo* [The Horseshoe Pub {because of correspondence, we know the date of her visit to be Tuesday, 3rd March 1964}]. That was an experience. I went in there with a girl from the hostel, a foreign girl, because I wouldn't go by myself because I was so nervous. I walked in and it was, 'Hello girlie. Who are you?' [Bindra always remembers Vernon Bell wearing, 'an old raincoat and driving an old car. He always wore this dirty old mackintosh, and he always came in that old jalopy']. So I produced my licence and said, 'I've come to join.' Everybody laughed and tittered and said, 'Oh yeah!' But they just humoured me. 'Oh yes, you can come back next week,' said Bell, which I did. [Bindra's (presumably second?) application for BKF membership was dated the 2nd March 1964, when she was nineteen years of age]. I went back with this girl, but she couldn't take it – one lesson was enough. I went back and joined. It was really strange. Whenever there was a person who didn't have a partner, my partner was taken off me because I was the lowest of the low. If anybody was late it was, 'Go in the corner and teach her.' That was the punishment, to teach me. In some ways I was segregated

The Horseshoe pub, Clerkenwell, where Bindra first started training with the London BKF club.

from the class on certain things even though I was just starting, even though there were other beginners there. Ignored, because I was a female.

'After about two weeks the novelty wore off and they thought if they treated me badly, I'd leave. But the worse they treated me, the more I was determined to stay. I think if they hadn't treated me so badly I would have left, but they got the opposite reaction. Virtually all the men treated me badly in a way. You know, you have two lines, and you bow to one another. They'd by-pass me, so there would be a gap, so they'd push the next one out of the way so I never had anybody opposite me. And then sometimes the instructor would shout, 'You opposite her – stay with her!' Jimmy Neal [a BKF London instructor who had joined in 1959] was very fair. I liked Jimmy Neal. After a while they began to accept me.' [After Sunday morning training at Upminster, Bindra would go back to Vernon Bell's house to complete some BKF typing].

'I always remember, I was so shy,' Bindra continued. 'I used to go to the Horseshoe club, change in the ladies' toilets, and look through the keyhole to see when the lesson started, so I wouldn't have to go out and talk to anybody. I'd hear the instructor say line up, and I'd go out. I was really shy. There were no women and the men, you know, thought, 'What is this thing amongst us?' Oh! It was terrible – a real male domain. It wasn't like that for one lesson – I was doing this for a year.'[21]

Bindra continued: 'I'm a Seventh Day Adventist, which is a very strict religion, and I didn't go to missionary college, I couldn't fit in, because all that was at the back of my mind was karate and training ... The Adventists didn't like me doing karate – they didn't understand it ... I don't know why, I just wanted to do it. After a while it just got hold of me. It was an escape; an escape from reality really, an escape from mundane things. It was a good release ... Karate gave me confidence. I used to get depressed, really depressed, very bad, and the only thing that brought me out of it was karate.'[21]

As Bindra's original application form may be lost, we are reliant on her London application form for details. Whilst she signed her BKF application form on the 2nd March 1964, as already noted, she didn't sign her Oath of Allegiance until the 13th March. She declared her hobbies as judo, karate, hiking and drawing. It seems evident that Bindra had indeed started karate before coming to London though, for this is not only stated on her form, when she refers to instruction received from Kidd at the Middlesbrough *dojo*, in Boundary Rd, but, also, in a letter to Bell dated the 2nd March 1964, when she noted that fees paid to the Middlesbrough club were reimbursed by Kidd. A reference to support her BKF application was provided by Miss R. Smith, Headmistress of Stainsby Girls' School, Middlesbrough, who wrote that Bindra 'was a girl of pronounced opinions and force of character. She had high moral standards.' The reference is dated the

```
                    THE BRITISH KARATE-DO FEDERATION.
                     (Affiliated to Japan Karate Assn)
National Sec./Organiser                              Chief Technical
  & Chairman                                           Adviser.
DR. V.C.F.BELL, Ps.D.,Ms.D.,                         TETSUGI MURAKAMI
  1 Dan Karate-Do        Application for Membership    1 Dan Karate-Do
  of J.K.A.                       as                    of J.K.A.
                         Full/Country/Associate/Member.
                                                 No...........
I, (Surname).LAVILLE...................(Christian Names)..Pauline...........
hereby wish to make application for membership of the above organisation and sub-
mit my personal particulars hereunder, for the perusal of the aforesaid Federation.
I confirm that all these particulars are correct and true in every respect, and I
agree, if accepted as a member of this Branch to obey and abide by its Rules and
Regulations, to uphold its Constitution, to conduct myself in a correct manner at
all times (both in and out of the Branch's premises) and to further uphold the
ideals and principals of the science of Karate as laid down by the B.K.F. and by
the J.K.A. by my personal example and co-operation at all times.
                    49 Glenedale Av  Signed................................
                         NW1           Witnessed............................
1. Surname.LAVILLE..................Christian Names.Pauline..........
2. Permanent address...............................................
3. Telephone No. (if any)..............3a. Married/Single...Single......
4. Age....19..............4a. Date of Birth.5/11/45..................
5. If under 18 years of age, have you your parents permission to join....-......
6. Hobbies/Interests..Judo,..Karate,..Hiking,..Drawing.............
7. Occupation..Typist...............
8. Service in H.M. Forces - a. period...............b. Service..-.........
   Rank....--...............Date of demobilisation...--......--......
(9. Condition of Health.Good..................9a. Examiner.Dr..Wheavell......
(10.Date of last medical.....................10a. Place of Exam.M'bro..........
(11.Have you any Heart/Lung trouble...........Details................
(12.Have you High/Low blood pressure...........................
(13.Do you suffer from any organic, mental or physical disabilities or weaknesses..
(.................................................................
14.State names and addresses of present Clubs or Societies which you belong to....
..M'bro..Judo..Club..............................
15.Outdoor/Indoor sports played..Judo..........................
16.Names/addresses of previous Karate Clubs.M'bro. Karate. Club,...........
17.Have you had previous Karate instruction.Yes...........a. by whom.Mr. F.
..Kidd..............Place.British. Karate. Fed, Boundry. Rd, M'bro.. Jonks.
18.Karate Belts held..None.........a. grade...-.........b. date of grading....
........-.......c. Examiner.......-............ .........d. Any further
   details of Karate experience..................................
19.Where did you hear of this organisation..Enquired.................
20.How and by whom were you introduced.By. Mr.. Kidd.. Class. Instruction...
21.State type of instruction desire - Private lessons.......Class Instruction.yep.
   Complete study of Karate.............(Answer Yes or No to above)
22.State precisely why you wish to learn Karate.Teacher, self defence, self
                                               control, self expression,
23.State how you became interested in Karate and what decided you that a Course of
   training would benefit you.Through. Judo. Useful, for. self. defense....
   In what way...Quickens. reflexes, alert. ness, and. mind.......
(Items Nos. 9 - 13 inclusive to be completed by your own Doctor and signed by
him, and he must also provide the intended Member with a note to say
"THIS MAN IS FIT TO PRACTICE KARATE".)
```

Pauline Laville's (Bindra's) application form to join the BKF

- 2 -

24. Having reached a standard in Karate, to what purpose do you intend using your knowledge. Means .of . self defence, ...
25. How do you think you can further the science of Karate and in what way........ By . supporting . the . Association, ...
26. Is your interest in this Branch and Karate as a whole -

    (a)Theoretical   (b) Practical ✓   (c) Philosophical   (d) Cultural ✓

    (e) Scientific   (f) Curiosity   (g) Knowledge ✓   (h) Sport ✓

    ....
27. For how long do you intend participating in Karate. As long as I am able...
28. Approx. days and time available for tuition. Any time.........................
29. Do you intend/desire to take Gradings in Karate. Yes...........................
30. How far in your studies do you intend to go. As far as I am able...........
31. Do you intend helping the Branch outside instruction hours... Yes..............

    If so how. Anything . that . is . required of me..........................
32. State briefly what your conception of Karate is. A . true . art of self defence
33. Name/Address of your Sponsor in joining this Branch - ....

    Mr.F.Kidd, British . K.Fed. J, Woodlands . Rd . New . Dorka.......
34. Name/Address of Seconder in joining...

    ....
35. I. Pauline . Laville. .agree to abide by my answers to the above details, and if for any reason I desire to resign my Membership I will do so in writing, stating my reasons, and giving at least one month's notice to the Branch Authorities.
36. I. Pauline . Laville......pledge myself at all times to keep and honour my written Agreements with the B.K.F. and by my integrity to keep all verbal and promised arrangements with this Branch forsoever as long as I am a Member.
37. I am fully aware and acquainted with the Constitution, Principles and Objects of the B.K.F. and with the full knowledge of them I desire to become a member. I declare that at all times during my Membership I will to the best of my ability fulfill my obligations as outlined in the Constitution.

    Signature. P. Laville....................Date. 2\March\64..............

    Sponsor/Witness.....................2nd Witness.... A. Oben...............

Return this form to:- V. C. F. BELL (1st DAN) of J.K.A.
          Chairman/Organiser
          of British Karate Federation.

          91, Perrymans Farm Rd.,
          Newbury Park, Ilford, Ex.
          Tel: Valentine 7705.

(To be completed hereunder by National   (To be completed hereunder by Branch
          Secretary)   Officer)

1. M/A/R sent. 6/3/64................. 1. Application. 7/3/63....
2. G/C sent 27/3/64.........No. 424.. 2. Refused..——..Accepted. 7/3/64...
3. LIC. issued... ✓..........516... 3. Interviewed. 9:30m...Time 7/3/64.
4. Full/Country/Ass.Member granted 7/3/64 4. Enrolled. 7/3/64........
          No. 713..... 5. A.F.Completed. 7/3/64....
5. "   "   "   " transferred..... 6. Fee paid. 3/3/64. Amount. 17/6.....
          Period.........   Resigned.........Cause.............
6. Enquiry Date...............   Dismissed.........Cause...........
7. Full details sent...............

Commenced 3m/B/c for Tuesday 24/3/64 paid £2-2-0 Dep.
LRF sent 1/11/64 ARF PL 16/2/65-   ARF '66 sent 14/12/65

BRITISH KARATE FEDERATION.

(affiliated to J.K.A., E.K.F., & YOSEIKAN)

Private and Class Pupil's Declaration and Oath of

Allegiance

I ..Partial..Laville............residing at Administration

.House...Flower.St,..London.W.C.)................

having been accepted as a Student Teacher/Private Pupil of
the B.K.F. to study the science of Karate and kindred
subjects fully realise, accept and swear on oath to abide
by, and promise to fulfil the following conditions
governing the Course(s) I shall be taught:-

1. To practice, participate and study all methods, tricks, movements at my
own risk, and to hold no one responsible but Myself for any injury sustained,
even if it should result in my death.

2. Never to abuse, misuse or publicise any of the knowledge I shall be taught,
as long as I live.

3. Never to use my knowledge of Karate etc., however trivial it may be to
the detriment, disadvantage or humiliation of a fellow human-being, as long
as I live.

4. Never to disclose, repeat, show or practice any method, trick or movement
I am taught to any person living, but to keep all my knowledge gained to
myself, realising it as a secret, deadly and dangerous art, and I learn it
only to protect my own life and family, as long as I live.

5. To use my knowledge only if, and when, my body or life is in danger, or
if my family is in danger, or to assist any unfortunate person attacked by
hooligans, drunkards, etc., or if I see any woman being assaulted and their
personage is in danger. Only then, will I use my knowledge of Karate, or
any infirm, aged or young person being attacked, and to use only sufficient
knowledge to render incapable the attack commensorate with the force of the
attack.

6. Never to appear in public to demonstrate, exhibit or teach, coach or
instruct any of the knowledge I am taught of Jujitsu, Karate or its kindred
branches to any person(s) classes, bodies, etc., until I am fully qualified
to do so, and then only with the written permission of my Tutor and or/my
parent Society, Federation or Association, as long as I live.

7. Never to bring dishonour, discredit, abuse or bad repute on my Tutor,
Society, my art of Karate, or on the science I am taught, by any bad con-
duct, loose behaviour, scandal, blasphemy, lies, drunkenness or in fact
by any dishonourable word, deed or action on my part, as long as I live.

8. To promise to always respect, honour and closely guard and protect all
the secret and deadly knowledge I shall be taught, as long as I live.

9. To promise to keep all my knowledge from the profane, violent, politi-
cally minded, agressive and abusive elements of mankind at all times, as
long as I live.

10. To uphold the name, honour, prestige and secret knowledge of my art,
my Tutor, my Society and my Federation by my own decent, moral chivalrous,
gallant and highest ideals of behaviour and example, as long as I live.

11. To respect the living, honour the dead, to respect and protect the
name, honour and personage of womanhood, and children at all times, as
long as I live.

12. To protect the weak, the infirm, the aged, the fearful and the lowliest
at all times from agressive, violent and abusive elements and circumstances,
as long as I live.

Continued........

Laville's (Bindra's) Declaration and Oath of Allegiance

- 2 -

13. To realise that any deviation, violation, infringement, breakage or abuse of any of my foregoing declarations, will result in full disciplinary action, compensation and retribution by the law of the land, by the Federation, by the Society and by my Tutor to the fullest extent possible.

14. To accept as final, absolute and fullproof any and all decisions by my tutor, Society or Federation on any matter governing the art of Karate and kindred sciences, as long as I live.

15. To realise that all the foregoing conditions, promises and declarations are binding and in force over my personage during my studentship, after graduation, after membership has ceased, in fact, as long as I live.

Pupil's Signature..P..*Saville*.....................

Date..13\March\64

1st Witness.......*L. Laville*.............

Address *Warwickshire. House. Gower. Str.. WrC.1*

2nd Witness...*M.. Olsen*.........

Address.*Warwickshire House, Gower St. W.C.1.*

Tutor...

Address...

B.X.F. Secretary/Official................

Address...

National Coach
  & Chairman
V. C. F. BELL.
3 Dan Judo
2 Dan Ju-Jitsu
2 Dan Karate-Do.

V.C.F. BELL. (2nd DAN)
  Chairman/Organiser
of BRITISH KARATE FEDN.
  The Horseshoe,
  Clerkenwell Close,
  E.C.1.

12th November 1963, more than two years after Bindra had left the school. Another reference (now lost) is referred to, and this was provided by Kidd, and covered other Middlesbrough women. This is further evidence then, that Bindra was training in BKF karate before moving to London.

Bindra's first grading was held under Bell on the 4th July 1964. Eleven London male students also graded to 8th kyu that day[22], including Michael Randall[23] and Raymond Fuller, both of whom hold the rank of 8th Dan at the time of writing. This is the earliest date that a woman is known to have graded in the BKF, as recorded in the BKF Grading Register. However, Bindra may not have actually been the first, as two other women are recorded as having been graded by Bell on the same day, at another *dojo* (see later).

'Later' [in 1965], Bindra recalled, 'I went to work at Butlins, and I stopped training for a while. I could have stayed longer but I missed karate, so I came back. I was in Minehead for two months and I taught karate to the kids. I think they only took me on because I said I'd done judo and karate. Once a week we did karate. Of course the kids hadn't seen it before and they asked about clubs, but there weren't any.'[24] We learn from a letter to Bell dated the 8th May 1965 that the date of Bindra's sojourn was from the 13th May 1965 for 'approximately six to eight weeks.'

Bindra continued: 'The people who tended to train were quite well off ... I remember Vernon Bell – we had to pay him monthly. I know that because I lived in a hostel – I wondered whether I'd have the money or not. Even if you were ill or went away, you still had to pay him ... I remember when I was going to Butlins, you had to put it in writing if you were going away, and he wasn't going to accept it. I said, 'Look, I'm going away,' [and he replied] 'Oh you'll have to pay when you get back.' I said, 'I can't pay,' [and he said] 'All right, girlie, all right. I'll let you off until you get back.' I had a hell of a struggle with him to let me off the fees.'[25] In a letter to Bindra dated the 27th July 1965, Bell notes that the sum owed was £5. 12. 6. It is known that the training fee, for *three* months (in advance), was £15.00 per person in 1964.

An interesting aside may be inserted here. By the summer of 1964, it was expected that Master Hirokazu Kanazawa of the JKA (see later) would teach for the BKF. In January 1961, he resided in Hawaii on behalf of the JKA and stayed until May 1963. One of his students was Miss Sue Largosa Reed, and she visited Bell and the BKF London *dojo* during the period 15th–18th July 1964. She had flown into

London from San Francisco and, after her short stay, caught a plane to Paris before continuing to Japan. Seven postcards to Bell from Sue L. Reed have survived. No doubt she gave a full account of BKF karate to Kanazawa when she reached Tokyo. General recollections from *karateka* who recalled her, was that she was a fine looking, dark-haired woman, whose karate was very good.

Bindra continued: 'I was always being asked out, and I went out with a lot of members, but nothing else, because I knew that if I had a liaison, something like that, with one of them, my karate was finished. I made a point right from the beginning not to get into bed with anybody, because they would all have talked about it, and I couldn't have done karate. So, I always went out, had a good time, and nothing else.'[24] 'Terry Wingrove and Brian Hammond [another BKF *karateka*] were the best of mates. Wingrove asked my sister out and I went out with Brian a couple of times.'[18]

It was during the Horseshoe pub *dojo* days that the numbers of students began to grow noticeably, and it was finally replaced by another *dojo* located at the Prince of Wales Baths, on the corner of Prince of Wales Road and Grafton Road, Kentish Town, NW5, in 1964. This change had become necessary because, as Bindra recalled, 'The landlord used to complain about the racket upstairs at the Horseshoe.'[24]

It was at the Kentish Town Baths, on the 6th November 1964, that Pathé Pictorial filmed a two minute fifty-two second colour piece on BKF karate and was screened for cinema audiences the length and breath of Great Britain. Unfortunately, whilst a number of latter day prominent faces appeared on the big screen, including Wingrove, Randall, Edward Whitcher, and Bindra's first husband to be, Raymond Fuller (who is seen breaking wood with a *gyaku-zuki*), Bindra is not amongst them and missed training that day, almost certainly due to illness.

In April 1965, Bell had organised for four JKA instructors – Taiji Kase, 6th Dan, and Hirokazu Kanazawa, Keinosuke Enoeda and Hiroshi Shirai (all 5th Dans, but placed in order of seniority) – to visit England as part of a JKA world tour and for Kanazawa to stay on for a year to teach for the BKF. Before taking part in a series of demonstrations that Bell had organised to help promote BKF/JKA karate, the instructors visited the new BKF *dojo* at Lyndhurst Hall, in Weldon Road, just off Grafton Road, Kentish Town. Bindra was training that evening and recalled three of the Japanese.

'I remember Kase because I thought, 'He's little, like me.'[18] 'I remember seeing Enoeda and thinking, 'He's nice.' I remember seeing Kanazawa, but I thought 'he's too young ...' and I wasn't impressed with Kanazawa – his slight build and boyish looks. I was used to older people.'[26]

Bindra, being one of the more senior and dedicated BKF students, took part in the London demonstrations along with Wingrove, Whitcher, Randall, Fuller, Robert Williams, Royston Merrick, Michael Peachey, Peter Labasci, John Johnstone, Jack Johnson, Christopher and Nicholas Adamou and, of course, the JKA instructors. All the evidence points to the conclusion that the first of these displays, at Kensington Town Hall, was the first time a BKF female student had demonstrated karate to the public. The date was 21st April 1965.

Michael Randall recalled: 'I remember the Kensington Town Hall demonstration ... About half-a-dozen of the students performed the *kata Heian Shodan* and *Heian Nidan*, plus we did some *gohon-kumite* to count, on the stage, as part of the display to show that people were practising karate in this country.'[27] Needless to say, the demonstrations held at Kensington Town Hall, Hornsey Town Hall (24th April 1965) and Poplar Town Hall (26th April 1965) were a great success.

Kanazawa, having been in England three months, held his first official JKA grading for London students on Wednesday 28th and Thursday 29th July 1965. The grading took place at the Lyndhurst Hall *dojo* between 7.00 p.m. and 10.00 p.m. each evening – the higher grades apparently taking their gradings on the Thursday. As Eddie Whitcher recalled: 'He [Kanazawa] took all of our previous grades away. 'When you grade under me, I will decide what you are worth' [Kanazawa said]' - (R. Butler).[28]

In a letter to a Mr. N. Bell (no relation), of Pendleton, Salford, that Vernon Bell wrote on the 15th November 1965, he noted that: 'All gradings from Mr. Murakami were rescinded when the BKF affiliated with the JKA last year and all persons holding grades from him have to be re-graded and re-examined by Mr. Kanazawa under the eight kyu training system of the JKA.'[28] It is true that whilst the vast majority of students graded upwards from their last Murakami grade (so Murakami's gradings may be regarded as having been very respectable), a few seniors, after their first Kanazawa grading, stayed on the same grade or were graded downwards. The fee for the grading was four shillings, if one was attempting 4th kyu or below, and ten shillings for 3rd kyu and above (though in the event of failure for a brown belt grade, six shillings was returned).

All grading students were required to complete an application form

Laville's (Bindra's) application to take part in Master Kanazawa's first London grading.

for grading. Grading students had to be present in the *dojo* fifteen minutes before the grading was to commence, in a clean *gi*. Every grading student was required to stay until the end of the grading, when the results were announced.

We are indeed fortunate that many of the actual forms have survived for this historic grading, with Kanazawa's notes on each student being evident. Grading forms exist for forty-four students residing in London or the Home Counties. The only woman present, Bindra, then an 8th kyu, successfully graded to temporary 6th kyu, thus grading one and a half grades. This is not, however, the first time

JAPAN KARATE ASSOCIATION.
(INCORPORATE BY CHARTER IN JAPAN)

GRADING APPLICATION

CLUB ...B.K.F...............

SURNAME *Miss* .LAVILLE............ FIRST NAME(S) ..PAULINE.........

ADDRESS ....GLAUSTER..AV;... DATE OF BIRTH .JAN..5...19../...
...GAMDEN.TOWN....

PREVIOUS KARATE EXPERIENCE ..12.YEARS.......

OCCUPATION ..TYPIST.........

EXAMINERS NAME ....

PRESENT GRADE	BASIC	FORM	KUMITE	TOTAL	RESULT	EXAMINERS REMARKS
8+" KYU	6	6	6 ✓	58	T. 6 KYU	

EXAMINATION FEE .... DATE OF EXAMINATION ....

AMOUNT RETURNED ☐

4th KYU & UNDER = 4/-

3rd KYU & ABOVE = 10/-. IF EXAMINEE OF 3rd KYU & ABOVE FAILS
THE GRADING, THE SUM OF 6/- WILL BE
RETURNED.

SHODAN = £2. 0.0. ON FAILING £1.10.0. RETURNED

NI-DAN = £2.10.0. ON FAILING £2. 0.0. RETURNED

SAN-DAN = £3. 0.0. ON FAILING £2.10.0. RETURNED

CERTIFICATES OF PROFICIENCY OF THE J.K.A. ARE AWARDED TO ALL GRADES
ABOVE 3rd KYU.

The results of Laville's (Bindra's) first JKA grading. The grading was held under Master Kanazawa whose comments, in Japanese, can clearly be seen – 28th July 1965.

a woman ever took a full JKA grading in the British Isles (see later). Twenty-four examinees passed grades below her, four graded with her, and eighteen graded above her.[29]

The JKA grading syllabus of the time reveals what Bindra and her fellow examinees would have had to do. As it is unclear, exactly what grading Bindra was attempting given the restructuring, though it is likely to have been 7th kyu, 8th kyu to 6th kyu will be provided:

Hachi-kyu (8th kyu) … white belt

1. Basic Techniques:

    a) *Zenkutsu-dachi, gedan-gamae* …. M.F [moving forwards] …. *oi-zuki*
    b) *Zenkutsu-dachi* at *hanmi* …. M.F…. *age-uke*
    c) *Zenkutsu-dachi* at *hanmi* …. M.F…. *shuto-uke*
    d) *Kokutsu-dachi, shuto-uke* …. M.F…. *shuto-uke*
    e) *Zenkutsu-dachi, gedan-gamae* …. M.F…. *mae-geri* with rear leg
    f) *Kiba-dachi* …. Crossing legs …. *yoko-geri-keage*
    g) *Kiba-dachi* …. Crossing legs …. *yoko-geri-kekomi*

2. *Kata – Heian* No. 1 [*Heian Shodan*]

3. *Kumite – Gohon-kumite*

Shichi-kyu (7th kyu) ... white belt

1. Basic Techniques

    a) *Zenkutsu-dachi, gedan-gamae* …. M.F …. *oi-zuki*
    b) *Oi-zuki* …. M.B [moving backwards] …. *age-uke*
    c) *Age-uke* …. M.F …. *chudan (soto) ude-uke*
    d) *Ude-uke* …. M.B …. *kokutsu-dachi, shuto-uke*
    e) *Zenkutsu-dachi, gedan-gamae* …. M.F …. *mae-geri*
    f) *Kiba-dachi* …. Crossing legs …. *yoko-geri-keage*
    g) *Kiba-dachi* …. Crossing legs …. *yoko-geri-kekomi*

2. *Kata – Heian* No. 2 [*Heian Nidan*]

3. *Kumite – Gohon-kumite*

Roku-kyu (6th kyu) … blue belt

1. Basic Techniques

    a) *Zenkutsu-dachi, gedan-gamae* …. M.F …. *oi-zuki, sanbon-renzuki*
    b) *Zenkutsu-dachi, gedan-gamae* …. M.B …. *age-uke, gyaku-zuki*
    c) *Gyaku-zuki* …. M.F…. *chudan (soto) ude-uke, gyaku-zuki*
    d) *Gyaku-zuki* …. M.B…. *kokutsu-dachi, shuto-uke*

e) *Zenkutsu-dachi, gedan-gamae* .... M.F.... *mae-geri*
f) *Kiba-dachi* .... Crossing legs .... *yoko-geri-keage*
g) *Kiba-dachi* .... Crossing legs .... *yoko-geri-kekomi*

2. *Kata – Heian* No. 3 [*Heian Sandan*]

3. *Kumite – Kihon ippon-kumite (choku-zuki* at *jodan* and *chudan,* each twice)

Kanazawa's second grading for London BKF members, again at the London Lyndhurst Hall *dojo,* was held on the 8th November 1965. On this occasion, Enoeda, and, possibly, Kase accompanied him. Bindra was successful in passing full 5th kyu along with six men, and thus she graded one and a half grades. Only eight men graded above her, yet thirty-seven men graded below her.[30] The grading she would have undertaken was as follows:

Go-kyu (5th kyu) ... purple belt

1. Basic Techniques

   a) *Zenkutsu-dachi, gedan-gamae* .... M.F.... *oi-zuki, sanbon-renzuki*
   b) *Oi-zuki* .... *M.B* .... *age-uke* .... *gyaku-zuki*
   c) *Gyaku-zuki* .... M.F.... *chudan- (soto) ude-uke, gyaku-zuki*
   d) *Gyaku-zuki* .... M.B.... *kokutsu-dachi, shuto-uke, zenkutsu-dachi, nukite*
   e) *Zenkutsu-dachi, gedan-gamae* .... M.F.... *mae-geri, ren-geri* at *chudan* and *jodan*
   f) *Kiba-dachi* .... Crossing legs .... *yoko-geri-keage, yoko-geri-kekomi*
   g) *Zenkutsu-dachi* .... M.F.... *mawashi-geri*

2. *Kata – Heian* No. 4 [*Heian Yondan*] .... [purple belt with a white strip]

3. *Kumite – Kihon ippon-kumite (choku-zuki* at *jodan* and *chudan,* each twice)

Kanazawa's third grading for London BKF members, held again at the same location, was conducted between 7.00 p.m. and 10.00 p.m. on Wednesday 23rd for 6th kyu and above, and Thursday, 24th February 1966, for 7th kyu and below. On that Wednesday, Bindra was successful in passing her full 4th kyu along with five men. Six men graded above her and forty-three men below her.[31] The grading requirements for 4th kyu are unknown.

Kanazawa's final grading at Lyndhurst Hall for the BKF, was held on the 20th and 21st April 1966. Information on this grading is sparse, yet it is highly significant, for on the 20th April, Edward Whitcher was

JAPAN KARATE ASSOCIATION.

(Incorporate by Charter in Japan)

GRADING APPLICATION.

CLUB. LONDON .KARATE. CLUB, ...

MISS
SURNAME. LAVILLE. . . . . FIRST NAME(S) PAULINE. (MISS) . . . .

ADDRESS. 49, .GLOUCESTER. AVENUE, ... DATE OF BIRTH. JANUARY 8th 1945. . . . . .

. LONDON .N.W.1. . . . .

PREVIOUS KARATE EXPERIENCE. . .2 .YEARS, ...

OCCUPATION. DICTAPHONE TYPIST, ...

EXAMINERS NAME. . Enoeda . . . Kanazawa ,

PRESENT GRADE	BASIC	FORM	KUMITE	TOTAL	RESULT	EXAMINERS REMARKS
6 Kyu (Temp)		5´	5´		5 KYU	

EXAMINATION FEE [10] - *pr uWell*, DATE OF EXAMINATION 8/Nov/6.5..:

AMOUNT RETURNED [ ]

    4th KYU & UNDER = 4/-.

    3rd KYU & ABOVE = 10/-.   IF EXAMINEE OF 3rd KYU & ABOVE FAILS
                                THE GRADING, THE SUM OF 6/- WILL BE
                                RETURNED.

    SHODAN = £2. 0.0.   ON FAILING £1.10.0. RETURNED

    NI-DAN = £2.10.0.   ON FAILING £2. 0.0. RETURNED

    SAN-DAN = £3. 0.0.   ON FAILING £2.10.0. RETURNED

CERTIFICATES OF PROFICIENCY OF THE J.K.A. ARE AWARDED TO ALL GRADES
ABOVE 3rd KYU.

49.

The results of Laville's (Bindra's) second JKA grading, under Master Kanazawa, on the 8th November 1965.

STATUS
Membership is recorded below.

Regd. No.	From	To	Fee Pd.	Status	Recorded	Authy
713	2/3/64 – 31/10/64				31/1/65	
	1/1/65 – 31/12/65				30/4/65	

Nal. License No. 424   Issued 2/3/64
Renewed (1) 424   1/1/65
         (2)
         (3)

OFFICIAL APPOINTMENTS

(1) Branch Committee............ period............
(2) Area Officer............ Authority............

Do not fold or mutilate this Card, which remains the property of B.K.F., and must be returned when membership expires. In event of loss or damage, a new Card will **NOT** be issued and Gradings witheld.

Member's Signature............

THE BRITISH KARATE-Do FEDERATION

INCORPORATING

KARATE CLUB OF BRITAIN

Directly affiliated to Japan Karate Assn. which is only body recognised by Japan Ministry of Education.

B.K.F. is only Authorised Organisation for Britain of J.K.O., Tokyo, for development and control of Karate-Do system of Funakoshi-Gichen.

Technical Director: H. KANAZAWA (5 Dan of J.K.A.)

National Sec./Organiser: V. C. F. BELL, PsD., Ms.D.
91, Perrymans Farm Road, Ilford, Essex.
Telephone: VAL 7705 (10 a.m.–5 p.m.)

(B.K.F. was founded in April, 1957, by official charter issued by Federation Francaise de Karate, Paris, to Mr. V. C. F. Bell)

DUPLICATE ISSUED 30/11/65

This is to certify that MISS P.E. LAVILLE
of 49 GLOUCESTER AVE, N.W.1.
has been duly enrolled as a FULL/HONORARY Member of this Federation as from 2/3/64
He/she has further been registered as an honorary member of the B.K.F. Affiliated Branch at London N.W.5 for the study and practice of J.K.A. system of Karate as from 2/3/64
This member is a Karateka of AMATEUR STATUS ONLY and his/her membership of this affiliated Branch at London N.W.5 and his/her approved registration with B.K.F. does not entitle this member to teach, represent or perform Karate in any manner outside or within the affiliated Dojo, only as a practical member to further his/her own Study of this Art of Karate. By his/her elected registration as a member of this Federation this member has accepted with Full awareness all obligations of membership of the B.K.F. and its affiliated Branches, under Statutes laid down by B.K.F. and its parent body. ONLY on these conditions is membership granted for periods stated.

OFFICIAL KARATE GRADING RECORD   4/2/64 7/3/64

KYU Grade	Awarded	Examiners	Place	N.G.R.	Authorised
NOVICE (Red)	2/3/64	Whell Loda	✕		2/3/64
HACHI 8th Kyu (White)	4/7/64	Whell Loda	489 15/9/64	Whell
SHICHI 7th Kyu (White)	28/7/65		Loda	466 30/11/65	Whell
ROKU 6th Kyu (Blue)	28/7/65 (TENT)		London	70A 566	30/11/65 Whell
GO 5th Kyu (Purple)	8/11/65		London	720	30/11/65 Whell
YON 4th Kyu (Purple)					
SAN 3rd Kyu (Brown)					
NI 2nd Kyu (Brown)					
ICHI 1st Kyu (Brown)					

Laville's BKF light blue membership card showing her gradings to 5th kyu

promoted to *Shodan* under Kanazawa. Application forms for this grading have survived for only twenty-one people[32], of which Bindra is one. Whether these students were the only people to grade is unknown, for entries for this grading do not appear in the BKF grading register. It is clear from what Bell wrote at the bottom of virtually all these forms, that most of these students were inactive BKF members on the 1st June 1966.

JAPAN KARATE ASSOCIATION.

(Incorporate by Charter in Japan)

GRADING APPLICATION.

CLUB.. London ....BKF.......

SURNAME. Laville................ FIRST NAME(S)..Pauline. (Miss).

ADDRESS..79, Gloucester. Ave... DATE OF BIRTH...Jan. 8. 8'.45...

.........London. NW1.....

PREVIOUS KARATE EXPERIENCE...2½ years..........

OCCUPATION. Dicta/Typist........

EXAMINERS NAME. MR....Kanazawa.....

PRESENT GRADE	BASIC	FORM	KUMITE	TOTAL	RESULT	EXAMINERS REMARKS
5	X '	4 '	4		4	

EXAMINATION FEE 10/- utell   DATE OF EXAMINATION .23/2/66....

AMOUNT RETURNED

4th KYU & UNDER = 10/-.

3rd KYU & ABOVE = 1/0/-.   IF EXAMINEE OF 3rd KYU & ABOVE FAILS
                             THE GRADING, THE SUM OF 1O/- WILL BE
                             RETURNED.

SHODAN   = £2. 0.0.   ON FAILING £1.10.0. RETURNED

NI-DAN   = £2.10.0.   ON FAILING £2. 0.0. RETURNED

SAN-DAN = £3. 0.0.   ON FAILING £2.10.0. RETURNED

CERTIFICATES OF PROFICIENCY OF THE J.K.A. ARE AWARDED TO ALL GRADES
ABOVE 3rd KYU.

H. G. Replied No 757 19/3/66 utell

49.

The results of Laville's (Bindra's) third JKA grading, under Master Kanazawa, on the 23rd February 1966.

It was during mid 1966 that a seismic rift occurred in the BKF that gave rise to the formation of the Karate Union of Great Britain. Bindra was in the thick of things from the outset. She recalled that the KUGB, 'did start in the South, contrary to what the Liverpool ... [lads] ... say ... The meeting took place in the pub [The Admiral Napier, in Kentish Town] and we all decided to form our association, and we wrote to Liverpool to see if they wanted to join. We started it. Eddie was definitely the head of it ... We'd had a letter back [from Liverpool] saying they wanted to run it from there, but we'd broken away [from the BKF] first and asked them if they'd wanted to join, and we sat in the pub discussing it. And they [the students sitting in the pub] said, 'Oh, let them do it.' I said you'll rue the day you ever did that. I remember saying that. And I tried as hard as I could to get them not to hand over the administrative power to Liverpool [and Manchester] ... but they handed over the administrative power we'd started in London.'[33] The formation, even who suggested the name, 'Karate Union of Great Britain,' is disputed, but it is a small point and one that need not be gone into here.[34]

Because of the rarity of female *karateka* at this time, the media focused upon Bindra. As an example of this, John Chisholm, a former BKF member who was now a senior student in the early KUGB, in London, worked as a rigger in the film industry at Elstree Studios. He also ran a karate club in Chiswick, and invited actors Lee Marvin and John Cassavetes to attend a class in an evening after filming, *The Dirty Dozen*, by day. Kanazawa and Enoeda put on a demonstration with some of the senior KUGB London members, including Bindra. She recalled: 'When he [Marvin] walked in, there was no fanfare or anything. He just sat with the crowd, three seats from the front ... watched the demonstration with John Cassavetes, and left. Marvin came up to me and said, 'Thank you very much. I really enjoyed that.' He was a lovely man ... Cassavetes just stood there smiling and nodding his head. Lee Marvin did all the talking.' She continued: 'I was the only woman, and the other thing I remember was all the photographers. Instead of the photographers going towards the men, they all zoomed in on me, and the men stood there thinking, 'What's this? They've come to see us.' But of course they'd never seen or heard of a woman doing karate.'[35] A good press photograph of Bindra performing *shuto-uke* that night does exist on a contact sheet, but from which newspaper the authors know not, hence its non inclusion here, but, almost certainly, one of the London dailies.

Bindra also ran, with Fuller, one of the most influential *dojos* in the country at this time. Bindra recalled: 'Kanazawa gave us so many weeks to find a hall or else he was going back to Japan.'[36] Chris Adamou, who worked up in the City as a solicitor's clerk, found the John Marshall Hall (a late Victorian church hall), in Blackfriars Road, south of the River Thames, near Blackfriars Bridge and underground station, during one of his lunch hours after two weeks, and his brother, Nick, paid for the first month's rent. Entry to the *dojo* was via a side entrance in Colombo Street, though the entrance was always approached through the church grounds from Blackfriars Road. The *dojo* was spacious and in good repair, the dark parquet flooring contrasted with the white walls and light wooden panelling surround.

Bindra recalled: 'When we moved into Blackfriars it was really exciting. It was a fantastic feeling, and the hall was so lovely ... the under floor was heated. It was brilliant – hot water pipes!'[37] Kanazawa recalled Blackfriars as being a 'nice *dojo*.'[38]

The *dojo* was the scene for spirited training for men and women alike. Bindra remembered training there: 'I had to compare myself with the men, and I think that did help, as opposed to nowadays when you've got other women, because it made you more determined. After I got to Blackfriars, I had my eye blacked, I got my nose smashed – blood everywhere. I think it was no holds barred, though some [men] would hold back.'[39]

'I had an aim. I wanted to be like the men ... I'd go mad if someone stepped in ... [and my male partner deliberately took it easier].'[18]

The Blackfriars *dojo* was visited by Bernard Braine, Tory M.P for South-East Essex in November 1966. Following a life sentence given at the Old Bailey to a certain Mr. Creamer, who supposedly killed a man in three seconds with about seven karate blows[40], Braine was to ask the Home Secretary for a government enquiry into karate and visited the club to get a taster of what was going on in the karate world. In a very short piece by an unknown journalist in the *Daily Express*, entitled, '*Pauline Puts Her Best Foot Forward – M.P. Sees Karate Session*,' the report begins: 'Blonde Pauline Laville [Bindra] last night showed an M.P. how to use karate blows if he was ever attacked ... [and that] Mr. Braine watched twenty-one year old Pauline ... and her friends demonstrate a series of complicated routines during a training session.' Accompanying this piece is a photograph by Express cameraman, John Downing, showing Bindra counter-attacking Fuller with a *yoko-geri-kekomi*, and with Kanazawa and Braine standing, watching in the background.

Bindra was a force to reckon with, especially if under stress. She

The Blackfriars *dojo*, where Bindra trained

recalled an incident that happened at the Blackfriars *dojo* shortly after, concerning a foreign female student who had joined the club. Names have been withheld in this and other stories, for it is the stories that may be relevant, not the people in them. Bindra continued: 'I remember smashing – [a female student] up in the Blackfriars toilets. We had a terrible bust up … Being foreign she thought she was superior … she really tried to show her superiority … My dad had died that day … and I just wasn't in the mood. She had a topknot on the top of her head like the Japanese wear with the chopsticks through it and I thought I'm going to have that off. I got hold of this topknot and just threw her. I didn't use karate; I just picked her up and threw her against the wall. I got all her clothes, bra and everything and threw them out the door. All the men … [were surprised] … she wouldn't get changed with me after that … she got changed under the stairs.'[18]

Bindra then recalled an incident along a familiar theme: 'An American girl came along too. This is when – [a here unnamed instructor] came … It was very early on. She came to the club; she was an *au par* or something. I remember her because she was the … [first] woman I ever saw training. I got on really well with her. She was a beginner. We were quite good friends. The next thing I knew she wasn't paying any *dojo* fees. This was in the Vernon Bell days and I remember going up to him and asking why I had to pay fees when she didn't. But — [the instructor] was apparently sleeping with her. I said to — [the instructor] what had she got that I hadn't got. I was just so naïve. I didn't realise it [not paying fees] was for that reason ... She always had her knitting with her. Whenever we went on a train, she always had her knitting. She was a big girl, heavy. What made her leave [the club] was when —- locked her in a room and went to a party ... you know, 'you stay here. I'll see you when I get back.' So he locked her in this flat, went to a party, came back and let her out, and that did it. I never saw her again. I realised then that if you slept around with these men your karate was finished. So I made a point of staying clear, avoiding [such people]. I never, ever went out with any of them, even though I could have done. I'm not being big-headed or anything, because they'd sleep with anything in a skirt, they were like that.'[18]

There was another tale along similar lines, that Bindra related. 'There was this girl in the club and — [a here unnamed student] was going out with her ... he really thought a lot of her. But — [a here unnamed instructor] said, 'You men must not have any women; it's wrong. You must dedicate your life to karate. Women are bad for you' ... One night — [the student] had reason to go to — [the instructor's] flat, and who should answer the door, but this girl in a dressing gown. This was like ten o'clock at night. And he asked her what she was doing there and she said that she was taking dictation, but I don't think anyone believed her. So for some people the myth vanished. Some people then started cottoning on to what ... [was going on].'[18]

Bindra also recalled: 'I remember walking down Oxford Street [with a here unnamed instructor]. We stopped by a fur shop and he asked whether I'd like a coffee and I said, 'yes please,' but I always kept my distance; I never fraternised ... [The instructor said], 'If I had a girlfriend I'd buy her a fur coat like that.' I said, 'I don't believe in killing animals for fur coats ... and then I went away. I wouldn't have any of it. With Ray Fuller it was different because you could tell if he was serious or not, but with things like that [the instructor] they'd love you and leave you.'[18]

Shortly after the Blackfriars *dojo* opened, a Hampstead doctor, Ralph Blair Gould, founded the *dojo* at Garth Hall, in Child's Hill, near Golders Green. On a Friday evening in October 1966, Tony Freeman, in an article, '*A Sport Called 'Art' – But Oh so Violent*,' in an unknown newspaper, gave an account of a two-hour 'ballet of violence' in Cricklewood by members of the Golders Green *dojo*. Dr Blair Gould started proceedings by giving a short talk to the assembled audience on the history, morals, values and benefits of karate training in modern society, and to dispel popular myth. Then the display began. Both Bindra and Nick Adamou were quoted in the article. Freeman described Masters Enoeda and Kanazawa as, 'Bamboo-hard, quicksilver fast and intensely concentrated, they showed themselves to be literally living weapons.'

Freeman considered the demonstration to be a 'disturbing, tense and – to be frank – somewhat ugly display of scientific and controlled violence,' but went on to say that there was 'an element of gentleness underlying their ferocity – giving the message that this dangerous art does perhaps foster self-restraint and responsibility.' In an interesting conclusion for that time, Freeman noted that karate is, 'a dangerous and anti-social art, wisely fenced in with the strictest rules and code of ethics by its controlling body. But, if I [Freeman] had teenage daughters, I WOULD teach it [karate] to them in these violent times.'

Bindra recalled in an interview of the 2nd February 1994, two post-1966 incidents that, whilst (not that far) beyond the remit of this book, shall be included because they seem relevant.

Once Bindra had attained the black belt grade, life was far from easy. She recalled: 'I remember a course at Crystal Palace and Enoeda said you're training with him [a certain Japanese instructor] … Some mats were put out and for two hours this Japanese hammered me, by myself, just to see how much I could take. Luckily, I'd done judo, so I knew how to fall, thank God, but he hammered me. I remember a chap, —, was disgusted, and he almost came out of the lesson. He said, 'I've never seen anything so disgusting in all my life.' To this day I don't now why Enoeda did [allowed] it.'[18]

Bindra continued: 'I also remember the first time a woman Japanese instructor came over to the course at Crystal Palace and Enoeda said, 'Right, all the ladies over there with her', and I thought, 'I'm really going to enjoy this.' And then he said, 'Except you! Stay where you are!' So he wouldn't really let me go with the other women … I took it as a complement.'[18]

Bindra noted the following three points about the benefits of her training. Firstly, 'Karate helped me make decisions;'[18] secondly, '[It also helps you to read people], that's your training. Because you try and read the moves, in *jiyu-ippon* or whatever, it suddenly comes and that's another asset [of training] I think … It's scary ... It's frightening in a way – the longer you stay in karate the stronger it gets;'[18] and, thirdly, 'I think martial arts, karate, brings out the simplicity … clean, Zen influence. It happens without you knowing it.'[18]

Bindra is exceptional and Seaton recognised this as soon as she started training. He recalled: 'In Pauline's early training days, I knew she was going to be a very high level *karateka*, and over the years since then she has proved that to be true. She has really turned out to be a top-level practitioner, first-class instructor and organiser, as well as promoting the self-defence and sporting aspects of karate on a national basis ... A very large number of people are practising and gaining the excellent physical and mental benefits of karate today because of Pauline's involvement and total commitment over the years.'[20]

Finally, Nicholas Adamou recalled an interesting episode that occurred at the Lyndhurst Hall *dojo*, presumably referring to either Bindra or Black (see later). He noted: 'One of the women students shouted out, 'Kanazawa *Sensei*!' and he literally stopped dead in his tracks as if he was waiting for an attack.'[41] But let us now return to Bindra's fellow Middlesbrough students from 1964.

Denise Bedford signed her BKF membership application form on the 27th December 1963, although her Oath of Allegiance wasn't completed until the 21st May 1964. Sixteen years of age and a coil winder by occupation, Bedford listed judo, dancing and sewing amongst her hobbies. She became interested in karate through her judo club and cited Bindra as the person who introduced her to it. Her application sponsor was Fred Kidd and her second witness, Walter Seaton. Her licence was issued by Bell on the 1st June 1964 and she paid a fee of seventeen shillings and sixpence. Whether she actually trained before she was accepted as a BKF member is unknown. Kidd also acted as her referee, writing that he had 'known Miss Bedford from childhood, and her parents were my neighbours up 'till the last seven years and were, and still are a good family of character. She is also a keen member of judo. Miss Pauline Laville will also be able to recommend her to you.'

Doreen Would signed her BKF membership application form on the 18th February 1964, when she was twenty-one years of age, single, and an upholsteress by occupation. Her hobbies were given as swimming, dancing, gardening and sewing, and she was a member of the Middlesbrough Judo Club, based at the Upton Social Club.

She was introduced to karate by Geoffrey Heywood, who had been training at the Middlesbrough *dojo* for over a year and a half. Would wanted to study karate for self-protection and exercise. Once again, her application was sponsored by Kidd and witnessed by Seaton. One of her referees, a certain J. Barrass, wrote that Would was, 'pleasant, truthful, honest and a good worker, mixing well with her work

Doreen Would (1964)

companions. She does not easily tire at any task she sets out to do, and is exceptionally keen on her chosen athletics.' Her second referee, whose signature cannot be read, noted that he/she had known Would all her life and could 'vouch for her integrity which is above reproach. She has a pleasant disposition and a very friendly nature. For some time now, she has been an ardent student of judo and has now developed a genuine enthusiasm for karate, for which art I have no hesitation in recommending her to any person as a pupil.'

Carol Tombs was only fourteen and still at school when she completed her BKF membership application form on the 21st May 1964. She is extremely unusual in being accepted into the BKF due to her age. She had been introduced to karate by Doreen Would, no doubt through Middlesbrough Judo Club, of which she, too, was a member. Her other hobbies included needlework and cookery; she also played tennis. A surviving reference, by the Rev. H. Marshall, noted that she was a regular churchgoer and that he was 'very happy indeed to commend her to you.'

The last female from the Middlesbrough *dojo* for whom a membership form survives is Rosemary Maine. She was a seventeen-year-old student of languages at the time of signing her BKF application on the on the 25th June 1964. She enjoyed tennis, gardening, swimming, yoga and hockey. She had become interested in studying karate after seeing it on television. A surviving reference by a retired schoolmaster, whose name is not clear, notes that he could

Carol Tombs (1964)   Rosemary Maine (1964)

'testify to her character, ability and personality, all of which I consider of high quality.'

With Murakami deemed out of favour and Bell not employing him for BKF courses and gradings after early 1964, the Middlesbrough *dojo* members, unhappy that they were no longer under Japanese tutorship, left the BKF to join Tatsuo Suzuki's Wado-ryu group. In 1964, Tatsuo Suzuki visited Britain and took up residence in January 1965, with his assistant, Masafumi Shiomitsu, arriving in August that year.

The change in affiliation and style obviously accounts for the fact that no BKF gradings were forthcoming from the Middlesbrough *dojo* after 1964. Whether Bedford, Would, Tombs and Maine graded in Wado-ryu is unknown. However, Seaton, who was awarded his Wado-ryu 1st Dan in April 1965 (along with three others), by Suzuki, did recall another woman *karateka* who was a founder member of his Hartlepool Karate Club, a Wado-ryu *dojo*, which was established in August 1966, and her name was Alwyn Ditchburn. He recalled: 'Alwyn's wide range of top quality karate abilities started to show in her very early years and because of my involvement with Pauline Laville's early karate training days, I appreciated Alwyn's potential very quickly. Over the following years, like Pauline, Alwyn proved she was a first-class *karateka* and went on to win a number of *kata* championships.'[20] Ditchburn 'was promoted to black belt, 1st Dan, Wado-ryu, in 1970.'[42]

Another three early female students of Shotokan came from Jack Green's BKF Blackpool *dojo*, two of whom applied for BKF

Jack Green, instructor to the BKF Blackpool *dojo*, who encouraged women students to train.

membership on the 17th June 1964 and the third on the 9th June 1965. The Blackpool club had been up and running a year when Green, a thirty-four year old motor engineer, accepted his first two female students.

Doreen Draper and Janet Dorothy Revill joined together. Draper was twenty-one at the time, declaring her occupation as an 'alteration hand', which, presumably, referred to dressmaking. Her hobbies were walking, dressmaking and reading. At the time of her application, she was a member of the Keidokwai Judo Club, Revoe Gymnasium, in Grasmere Road, Blackpool, and she noted that she had already received karate instruction from Green, then a 4th kyu, at the said gym. She wished to learn karate for self-defence and to practise on Tuesday and Friday evenings for a total of four hours. Her only known reference comes from a member, almost certainly the minister, of Cavendish Road Congregational Church. Unfortunately, the reference in the authors' possession is partial and blurred. However, the referee noted that Draper was 'a young lady of exemplary [—and—] disposition, very conscientious in all she undertakes' and was 'a very esteemed member of the church.' The referee continued: 'Knowing Miss Draper as I do – not the slightest hesitation in recommending – for the post she desires, as I am absolutely convinced that she will give entire satisfaction.' Her Declaration and Oath of Allegiance had been signed on the 19th May.

Doreen Draper (1964)   Janet Revill (1964)

Revill was sixteen years of age at the time of her BKF application, and a shop assistant by occupation. Her hobbies were oil painting, reading, collecting records and ten-pin bowling. She also liked to play tennis and table tennis. Unlike Draper, she was not a *judoka*, nor had she had any experience of karate, though, like Draper, she had heard about karate through a newspaper and wished to learn for self-defence purposes.

Her Declaration and Oath of Allegiance had also been signed on the 19th May. Her referee was the manager of Boots the Chemists, a certain individual whose signature is quite unreadable. He wrote: 'During Miss Revill's employment with us, we have found her to be a trustworthy and pleasant mannered young lady and I am sure she will make a suitable member of your organisation.' Like Draper, her application was sponsored by Green and her second witness was D. Taylor. There were actually four Taylors training at the Blackpool *dojo* at the time, but none of them have the initial 'D', so who acted is a mystery.

Draper and Revill are entered in the BKF Grading Register as having graded under Bell, in Blackpool, on the 4th July 1964, the same day, readers may recall, as Bell graded Bindra in London. There is most likely to have been an error in recording here and we are therefore unlikely ever to know whether Bindra or the Blackpool *karateka* should appear in the register first. Draper and Revill are actually entered first, Nos. 486 and 487, respectively, with Bindra [as

Laville, of course] recorded as Nō. 489, but as the date is the same, the order is meaningless. Unfortunately, the surviving correspondence between Bell and Green is minimal and what there is throws no light upon the matter. Date entries in the BKF Grading Register are not always accurate.

Bindra, Draper and Revill are the only BKF female *karateka* registered as having graded in the BKF Grading Register to the summer of 1966. Draper is known to have at least reached 4th kyu, whereas Revill appears to have graded only the once, to 8th kyu. In fact, Draper and Bindra alternated as to who was the senior BKF female *karateka*, in terms of actual grading date – 8th kyu aside, when the JKA gradings took place, Draper led at temporary 6th kyu (grading on the 24th June 1965), Bindra at 5th kyu (when Draper graded on the 9th November 1965) and Draper at 4th kyu (grading on the 10th February 1966). The point is not purely an academic one, for Draper can thus claim the distinction of being the first woman to be graded by a JKA instructor in the British Isles (assuming the date entry is correct).

Like Bindra, Draper was graded 8th kyu by Bell, 6th kyu and 5th kyu by Kanazawa. Unlike Bindra however, Enoeda graded Draper to 4th kyu.

Draper attended the BKF Lilleshall Summer School based at the C.C.P.R. Recreation Centre, Lilleshall Hall, Lilleshall, Shropshire, from the 28th August to 4th September, 1965, under Kanazawa.

Kenneth Roebuck of the Rotherham BKF *dojo*, as Area Officer, attended a meeting at Bell's home on the last weekend in August 1964. A letter from Roebuck to Bell, dated the 2nd September, noted various motions carried at the meeting understood to be correct by Roebuck. One of these was that women and children be allowed to train at the Area Officer's discretion. This item was amongst a number of changes, but, as we have seen, women had been training, and encouraged to train, for the past seven years. Perhaps Bell was no longer vetting potential women's applications and their acceptance as BKF members was based purely on the Area Officer's recommendation.

The third Blackpool female member was Wendy Varley. She was twenty-one at the time of signing her BKF application form on the 9th June 1965 and was a typist. She declared being a member of the Keidokwai Karate Club, yet answered 'No' to the question, 'Have you had any previous karate instruction?' This is curious, for she later gives her karate experience as being 'eight months.' She had heard of the BKF through the karate club, having been introduced by Frank

Wendy Varley (1965)

Lomas. Lomas, at the time, was a twenty-year-old fitter who held the 6th kyu grade. Her application was sponsored by Green and her second witness was Alan Stewart, a senior at the club, aged twenty at the time and an engineer by occupation. Any references to accompany her application have not survived. Like Draper, Varley also attended the Lilleshall course.

Nicholas Adamou also attended the Lilleshall course and recalled: 'I do remember them [Draper and Varley] and can only say that, in my opinion and from what I remember about them, they were very soft and not dynamic or expressive at all in their karate techniques.'[43] In fairness, however, it must be remembered that Varley, at least, had been training less than three months at this time.

Varley was one of four female BKF students to have joined in 1965; the remainder were two from the Manchester *dojo* and one from the York *dojo*.

Carol Ashley Banks signed her BKF application form to join the Manchester *dojo* on the 4th March 1965, having been introduced to karate by her husband, Thomas. Thomas Banks, at twenty-four years of age, declared his occupation as company director, and had signed his BKF application form on the 11th January that year.

Carol was twenty-three years old at the time of becoming a karate student and was a housewife who enjoyed painting, swimming, walking and motoring (the last two of which her husband also declared an interest in). Terry Heaton, the Manchester *dojo* instructor,

Doreen Draper (first row, sitting, extreme left) and Wendy Varley (second row, fifth from left) attending the Lilleshall Hall Summer School: 28th August – 4th September, 1965. A number of well-known British *karateka* to be are also present, including Nick Adamou (back row, third from left) and Chris Adamou (middle row, extreme right), both from London, and, in the front row, starting second from left: Ian MacLaren (York), Steve Cattle (York), Andrew Sherry (Liverpool), Alan Smith (Liverpool), and, to Master Kanazawa immediate left, Ken Roebuck (Rotherham).

Carol Banks (1965)   Margaret Abbott (1965)

sponsored her application, with E. Bench acting as second witness.

The second of the Manchester *dojo* female students was Margaret Abbot, who signed her BKF application form on the 5th March 1965, having also been introduced to karate by her husband, Barrie. Barrie Abbot, at twenty-three years of age, was a structural engineer by profession, and had signed his BKF application form on the 1st November 1964.

Margaret, at the time of her BKF application, was a twenty-two year old aerodynamicist and a member of the Royal Aeronautical Society in London. She had first heard about the BKF from the woman's magazine, *She*. Bench sponsored her application, with Heaton acting as second witness.

The last female member to join the BKF in 1965 was Lesley Mary McLaren, of Gordon Thompson's York *dojo*, who signed her application form on the 27th August. She, too, had been introduced to karate by her husband, Ian. Ian McLaren had signed his BKF application form on the 14th April that year, and was working as a draughtsman and illustrator for the Civil Service. At the time, he was twenty-three years of age.

The BKF York *dojo* seemed to have used an abridged application form and not much information is available on Mary, as she was known. She was twenty years old at the time of her BKF application and a housewife.

Gordon Thompson, instructor to the BKF York *dojo*, who encouraged women students to train.

However, in an unknown newspaper by an unknown writer, a short article entitled, 'Karate Masters Show York How,' we see a photo of MacLaren performing a left *jodan empi* on Master Enoeda, with Master Kanazawa at her other side. The picture was taken on the evening of the York club's dinner at the Apollo Room, and all three are so attired. The date of the photo is probably late 1965 or 1966.

Similarly, women's use of self-defence was featured in an unknown Yorkshire newspaper by an unknown reporter of unknown date (though late 1966), with nurses training in the recreation hall of the City Hospital, York, under members of the York *dojo*. Entitled, 'Lest They be Molested ...' Three photographs are shown of two nurses, Judy Almond, performing a *teisho-uchi* on Walter Knowles and Eileen McDonald throwing Patrick O'Donovan, whilst nurse Ashby performs a *jodan-empi* on Neil McDonald under the watchful eye of Mary McLaren. It was stressed in the article that nurses, who walk the streets early in the morning and late at night, were being given the opportunity to learn self-defence.

To what extent the nurses were being taught self-defence *per se*, as opposed to Shotokan, the authors are unsure, however, Almond, McDonald and Ashby were practising after the KUGB was formed and the authors do not have any further details.

The self-defence course seems to have paid off for, in an article by an unknown reporter in an unknown newspaper, Ian McLaren, in an

Mary and Ian McLaren shortly after they had started training at the BKF St. Clements *dojo*, York – 1965.

article entitled, 'Dangerous in the wrong Hands,' is quoted as saying, 'I can't see anything ugly about karate. We even started a women's class with six members. There are only two regulars now – my wife Mary and Eileen MacDonald, a student nurse at the County Hospital.' The title of this report comes from the murder of a London barman, supposedly by the use of karate blows, and is the same case as noted earlier with regard to Braine's visit to the Blackfriars *dojo*. The case was famous and the article can be dated to October or November 1966. Mary is noted as being a green belt (6th kyu) at the time.

Of MacDonald, Thompson recalled: 'I remember Eileen MacDonald, vaguely. She was a small lass and I think she had to leave after a while because she was studying to be a nurse and could not spare the time.'[44]

Another two photographs exist showing Mary McLaren in action. The first, by an unknown photographer from an unknown newspaper, shows her performing a *chudan yoko-geri-kekomi* to her husband's lunging two-handed grasp, whose age is given as twenty-three. If this is correct, then the photograph was taken after, but including (given Mary's BKF joining date), August 1965. The second, also by an

Mary MacLaren, kneeling, second left, at the St. Clement's Church Hall *dojo* of the BKF York club (1965). To Mary's left is famous *karateka* to be, (the late) Steve Cattle. Back row, extreme left is Gordon Thompson; third from left is Mary's husband, Ian.

unknown photographer from an unknown newspaper, shows Mary striking with a right *shuto* to her male opponent's neck. She is given as twenty-two years of age, so if this is correct, then we can date the photograph to after, but including, December 1966.

Gordon Thompson recalled Mary McLaren: 'She was a wild one was Mary. If you gave her an inch she'd thump you one and would try anything.'[45] He continued: 'Ian and Mary volunteered to look after Mr. Kanazawa when he came to York and he got himself quite dug in there. He had a happy time stopping there … Mary had left the club just before I came back from South Africa when they got divorced.'[45]

Later, Thompson noted: 'Mary McLaren … was an independent spirit and quite a fiery character at times. I cannot recall anything particular about her [other than] she was a good club member and joined in nearly all the club activities. I think she rose to the rank of 3rd kyu, but I am not too sure about this, after all, memories forty years old are not too reliable. She was a pretty good technician as the standards of that time go, but nothing outstanding.

'[Kanazawa] sometimes turned up on their [Ian and Mary McLaren's] doorstep unexpected and unannounced at the beginning of the week and she took it all in her stride. She also got something of a reputation for chivvying him about a bit … 'It's time to get out of bed!' etc. After training and after leaving the pub ... [club *karateka*] were always invited round for coffee and she seemed to enjoy this very much.'[44]

The BKF had three *dojos* in Scotland during the first ten years of its history. The first (1961-1963), in Auchen Larvie, near Saltcoats, Ayshire, was run by Edward Ainsworth and had eleven known members; the second (1963-1966), in Aberdeen, was run by John Leeds Anderson and had forty-two known members; and the third (1964-1965), Dundee, was run by William McGuire and had sixty-one members. Of the one hundred and fourteen BKF Scottish members, not one is female, and there is no record of any female *karateka* in correspondence.

However, both McGuire and Anderson made enquiries about the possibility of enrolling women students. In a letter to Bell dated the 14th November 1964, McGuire wrote: 'I have had quite a few ladies asking if they could enrol with the BKF.' In an undated reply, Bell noted: 'Regards the ladies enrolling in the BKF, this is quite permissible … with a proviso that they will train separately as a group under you, but on the same system and methods, excepting in a much softer manner. Their fees will be the same.'

Similarly, in a letter by Bell to Anderson, dated the 13th December 1965, it is evident that Anderson had enquired in an earlier, now lost letter of the 7th December, about the possibility of running a women's karate class, and asked both Kanazawa's and Bell's views on this. Bell replied: 'Regards training for women, Mr. Kanazawa is in favour of this, but they should be kept separate from men unless you have no facilities for a separate class. BKF membership has been opened to women for the past year [which is contrary to evidence presented here], but in the other BKF *dojo*s most of the area officers include them in the men's classes.'[46]

The BKF *dojos* in Wales, at Newport (1963–1964), and Swansea (1965–1966), run by Michael Benson and Warren Scott, respectively, with nine and eight members respectively, likewise had no women members.

It was in early 1966 that the first BKF students gained their JKA black belts. On the 6th February [– licence date, the 10th appears on the JKA diploma[47]] that year, Andrew Sherry and Joseph Chialton of the BKF Liverpool *dojo* graded to *Shodan* under Enoeda. According to the BKF Grading Register, Jack Green likewise graded to *Shodan*, under the same examiner, in Blackpool, on the 11th February. It wasn't long after, that James Neal [also February[47]] (who, readers may recall was Bindra's instructor, along with Wingrove) and Edward Whitcher (20th April), both from the London *dojo*, would gain their black belts too. A number of Liverpool and London students followed over the

Suzanne Black (1966)

next nine months, and included in the latter group were Williams and Fuller. Although beyond the remit of this work, it is believed that Bindra was awarded her JKA *Shodan* towards the end of 1967, making her the first woman so graded in the British Isles.

The remaining three BKF female *karateka* commenced training in 1966. In the middle of the that year, as has been previously noted, many BKF clubs left to form the KUGB and BKF registration was not always followed leading up to this period. In other words, there may have been more than three females training in BKF karate up to the breakaway. However, we have what we have, and each application shall be dealt with by application form signing date.

On the 19th February 1966, Suzanne Black signed her application form to study karate at the London *dojo*. At this time, she was a twenty-five year old chemist's assistant. Her hobbies were painting, dancing, reading, poetry and sculpture. She had been introduced to the club by Jasper Lassey (a twenty-nine year old foreign service officer with the Ghanaian diplomatic service, who held the rank of temporary 4th kyu at the time), and she wished to improve her mind and body through practising the art, and gain peace of mind. No references exist for Black and no further information is available.

Bell wrote to a certain Mr. Humphreys at the Central Council for Physical Recreation (a forerunner of the Sports Council) on the 4th March 1966, to apply for recognition as the 'official body for

Shotokan karate for this country.' This is an important letter, Bell, wishing to work hand-in-hand with the CCPR 'to present Karate-do as a safe sport and a pleasurable hobby to be practised by young and old of both sexes, safely, and with enjoyment, and to free the name of karate from the tabs that have been placed on it as a killer sport, a super-normal art, and a lethal defensive Japanese blood sport, and in its place establish it as a form of physical education second to none, and on a par with and alongside judo and other sports.'

By 1966, the media were beginning to take more of an interest in the woman's angle to karate, or at least to feature them in photographs and quote them in articles – we have seen both Bindra and McLaren, for example. Tricia Manners, in the last of three articles on women's self-defence, entitled, 'Chop Him Down to Size,' which appeared on page 18 of the *Romford Recorder* on Thursday, 17th March 1966, described karate training at the Ben David Judo Club. Interested readers were advised to contact Leonard Palmer ({b. 1920} a television engineer by occupation), the secretary to the All-British Karate Association. Two photographs accompany the piece – one shows Manners kicking *mae-geri*, but clearly indicates she does not have a sound knowledge of karate technique, and the other has her thrusting her thumbs to her obliging male opponent's neck. There are some nice lines too, such as, 'you don't have to be dressed to kill,' and, 'kicking techniques are useless if you are wearing a tight skirt.' Interestingly, Manners wrote that whilst the club had received enquiries about training for women, it 'cannot cater for women.' The ABKA was established long after the BKF, and the authors know little about it.

Joan Shaw signed her BKF application form on the 12th April 1966. A twenty-nine/thirty year old housewife, she completed a much abridged application form from which little can be gleaned. With the club instructor and area officer being Leonard Moss, a forty-seven year old driver, and the witness being A. Deakin, it is possible to place this application with the Stoke B *dojo*. There had been an earlier Stoke *dojo* (Stoke A). Ironically, Shaw was the name of the BKF instructor at Stoke A, but the addresses differ – though, of course, the Shaws' could have easily moved in the intervening six years.

The last woman to have joined the BKF for whom a record has survived, before the formation of the KUGB, is Janet Esther Brannen. She signed her BKF application form on the 7th July 1966, when she was twenty years of age and a wages clerk by occupation. She, too, completed the abridged form and little is known about her, other that

Janet Brannen (1966)

she wished to train at the Bath *dojo* run by Brian Middleton.

The BKF Bath *dojo* was indeed small, and only six members are recorded in all, along with Middleton. In a letter to Bell by Bath member, Larry Vincent, dated the 23rd November 1966, we learn that 'due to our rigorous training schedules, two of the six members decided to 'drop out.' The members in question are Miss. J. Brannen and Mr. D. Parkes.' So, Brannen trained for only some four months.

When the KUGB was formed in 1966, they too were happy to accept women trainees. In an undated circular, though before the 9th September 1966, Terry Heaton, who became National Secretary of that organization, wrote: 'It is the object of the Union to bring karate to the attention of a larger public, as a sport which is able to be enjoyed by persons of all ages, regardless of sex.'

Whilst the KUGB began its national championships in 1967, it wasn't until 1973 that women were allowed to enter, and then only for *kata*, when seven took part (though, of course, this grew in the years to come). It wasn't until 1984 that there was a *kumite* event specifically for females, when forty-two entered.

The last entry in this book goes to Dorothy 'Dot' Naylor. She joined the Liverpool Red Triangle *dojo* during a very difficult period for the BKF and her details were never submitted to Bell, and so they remain unrecorded in the BKF archive. The Liverpool *dojo* left the BKF at the end of April 1966, one month after she became a member.

Dot Naylor (1978)

Dot (née Pemberton) was born in Rainford, Lancashire, on the 19th June 1933, one of eight children, to a mechanic. When she left school, she became a coil winder in a local factory, before marrying Charles Naylor in October 1955. Charles was a founder member of the BKF Liverpool *dojo* in 1961 and so Dot was exposed to karate early on. She recalled: "My husband just thought about karate all the time – day and night, and still does. In those early days, he kept going out in the evenings, I didn't understand, and I was seriously worried that he was having an affair.

"The early Liverpool *dojo* never had much money and so when Vernon Bell and Tetsuji Murakami came up, they stayed at our three-bedroom house in Arnian Road, Rainford. That would have been in 1962 and 1963. I can't say that I warmed to Bell. I found him egotistical and an eccentric character. I didn't know anything about karate, but when I spoke to him on other subjects, he always thought he knew something about everything.

"The first time I saw Murakami I was amazed at how small and lightweight he was. I'm five feet seven and a half inches and I was looking down at him, or at least that's how it appeared, which was unusual. [Murakami was five feet five inches in height and weighed nine stone]. But he was a lovely man. I know that in the *dojo* he was a terror, but outside, privately, he was a real gentleman. He was very good with the children and seemed to play with them quite naturally. He was also a fantastic dancer with wonderful hip movement. He'd dance with the children and he danced with me quite a few times in the kitchen too. I'm fond of dancing and I'm telling you he was really excellent. We'd dance to jazz, the Beatles, do the twist, whatever was popular at the time. I also remember that he'd eat anything that was put in front of him, though I liked to do him proud.

"When they came to stay, perhaps a couple of times a year, the two children we had would come and sleep in our room and Bell and Murakami would have a bedroom each.

"There were no women training in Shotokan karate in the Liverpool area at this time and it wasn't until I saw the demonstration given by *Senseis* Kase, Kanazawa, Enoeda and Shirai at St. George's Hall in April 1965, that I had any idea that I wanted to do karate. The display was truly amazing, though I thought quite vicious in places. I was sitting in the front row and Enoeda and one of the other Japanese were sparring. They were coming extremely close and, suddenly, this other Japanese stepped to the side allowing Enoeda's punch to fly past. Well, it stopped right in front of my face. It could have killed me, seriously. Enoeda looked at me and just laughed. I was just taken aback and I thought, 'I've just got to learn this.'

"Well, I asked Charles about starting and he said that women didn't go to the Red Triangle *dojo*, and so I asked him to teach me, but he refused, and that was that, at least for a while. But I thought, 'men have no right to tell women what they can and cannot do.'

"When Enoeda came to stay with us, I mentioned to him in conversation that it was a shame I couldn't train in karate and to my amazement and delight he replied that I could. The club must have advertised for a ladies class, because four of us turned up. I remember, now, that I encouraged a girl who used to baby sit for me to come and join us. But she didn't last very long. She was one of these women who thought, 'Oh, I'm feminine. I don't do things like that. Her attitude was, 'Well if a man hits me, I'll let him.'

"As I drove to that first lesson I thought, 'Oh my god, what have I got into?' Stepping into that *dojo* for the first time was like walking into school on your first day, the same kind of terrible feeling.

"Andy Sherry, who'd just received his black belt, taught us. When we first started training, all we ever did was stay on the spot because there wasn't enough room. When I mentioned this to *Sensei* Enoeda, he said, 'That's the way we train in Japan, on the spot.' I said I couldn't believe that, I thought you'd be all over the place.

' "No," he answered, "we train on the spot until we get it right and then we start moving." ' Some people thought it was a punishment to train on the spot, but it wasn't.

"*Sensei* Enoeda said to me that karate is best when the basics are correct. Of course I didn't understand at the time and he said that if you stick a pyramid on its apex, it will fall down, but if you turn it the other way around, what have you got? That's what you make your karate, the flat base. I have never gone back on that advice.

"The men would watch from the stage and I just felt so conspicuous, so embarrassed. I once heard a remark from one of the men, when we were doing *kata*, that we looked like fairies.

"The Liverpool Red Triangle was, I thought, a bit of a dump, and we had to change in the ladies toilet. My *gi* was made of two parts of course, a jacket and trousers, except that one part was given to me by Enoeda, the other by Kanazawa. They wrote on my belt in Japanese and I embroidered over the calligraphy. I lent that belt to someone but I never got it back.

"I thought the training and teaching at the Red Triangle were brilliant. I remember the names of two of the other three girls, Marilyn and Sheila. I loved the *kihon*, but the karate practice was physically demanding and it saw the other girls off, though I think Marilyn graded with me the first time. I drove the sixteen miles from Rainford to Liverpool twice a week and I started to really get into training. When I graded [12th July 1966] under Enoeda the first time, I was frightened to death, but I double graded to 8th kyu and then I graded to 7th kyu three months later (18th October 1966). I've always found karate gradings terribly frightening experiences and that's why I never graded beyond 3rd Dan [Naylor received her 1st and 3rd Dans from Enoeda on the 26th February 1970 and 15th September 1978, respectively].

"When the other girls left, I was the only woman, so I had to go in and train, and grade, with the men. The first time I trained with them, I had no confidence and I thought I'd hide in the back line. The trouble with this strategy was that the lines turn of course, so I was in the front line half the time!

"There was no difference in my training compared with that of the men. In fact, they were quite aggressive. I think they liked the idea of me retaliating. The men were really nice to me though, nobody ever refused to pair up with me, but I know that a few thought I shouldn't be there. These were different times and they felt I should be at home with the children and not have a couple of evenings out. The children, Jane and Mark, were seven and five, respectively, when I started training, but they were with Charles, who trained at his *dojo* in St.Helen's on different evenings, so it was not a problem.

"Some people feel guilty about leaving their kids, family, to go training. But what you have to remember is that you have a life as well. And the kids will be admiring you when you get older. You'll keep a

GRADE	DATE PASSED	EXAMINER(S)
9 KYU	12/7/66	榎枝慶之輔 K. Enoeda
8 KYU	12/7/66	榎枝慶之 K. Enoed
7 KYU	18/10/66	榎枝慶之輔 K. Enoed

Dot Naylor's 9th – 7th kyu grading entries in her KUGB licence

nice figure; you'll always be fit and alert.

"At this time other women thought I was daft – all that hard work, and for what? But, at the end of the day, you do get something. I honestly think from that day to this, that starting karate was the best thing I ever did, and the hardest. But if I was given a penny for every time I was told women shouldn't do karate, I'd be rich.

"I'll tell you the way things were then. When I passed my black belt grade, somehow a local newspaper found out about it. They wanted to interview me and take some photographs. I was quite proud of what I'd achieved and so I said I would be happy to do it. When the reporter and photographer arrived, they brought a large cake with them and I thought that was really nice. However, they wanted me to put my *gi* and black belt on and then take a picture of me cutting the cake with a *shuto*. Tied to the kitchen with my black belt you might say. They just didn't understand. Perhaps they thought it was a bit of harmless fun to sell their newspaper, but I refused to do it.

"The two students who stood out when I started, in my opinion, were Terry O'Neill and Bob Poynton. They were fantastic then, let alone later!

"Kanazawa would stay with us as well. He is a gentleman. I remember that he would eat fruit for breakfast and until midday. For lunch he'd eat vegetables and fish, perhaps a little meat, and then go for a run in the afternoon. He had a fantastic physique and his karate and his fitness were his life.

"Enoeda was different and would eat you out of house and home.

He stayed with us many times and would play with the children. Jane would actually call him 'Daddy Number 2.' Later, Charles was his best man at his wedding. Do you know that when Charles lost his job and we were very worried about where the next penny was coming from, Enoeda sent us two hundred pounds, which was a great deal of money in those days. We said that we couldn't possibly accept it, but he insisted. These were very happy times, and I miss *Sensei* Enoeda dreadfully. He was just wonderful, he had no right to die; I could hit him for doing it. His death was such a blow to Charles and myself, and a day doesn't pass without us thinking of him.

"I think Shotokan is wonderful for women, I really do. I hurt my hip badly some years ago, when I was in my sixties, after landing awkwardly from jumping down from a wall. I had to have a hip replacement. Afterwards, the surgeon, a very nice Indian gentleman, said that I had very interesting muscles around my hip and that the muscles kept tightening around the implements during the operation. He told me they had to give extra muscle relaxant. He asked me what I did in life and I told him that I was a postwoman.

"'No,' he replied, 'it's not that,' and he enquired further. Eventually, I was obliged to tell him that I trained in karate and had done so for more than thirty years. He then asked if he could train at the club and he began shortly after with his son. Unfortunately, he injured his fingers and decided to pack up. An orthopaedic surgeon needs his fingers, so I suppose he just felt he couldn't risk damaging them any further."[48,49]

The remit of this short book has been to cover the women who are known, and assumed to have trained in Yoseikan/Shotokan karate and the Shotokan of the JKA over a ten year period to 1966, through the BKF. Bell and his association appeared to be by far the largest player, at least up to 1965, yet there was at least one other British man teaching Yoseikan based karate, and his name was Martin Stott, of Manchester. Stott had trained in Paris under Tam-Mytho and is believed to have taught karate from 1961, but whether he encouraged or trained women students is unknown.

With regard to Shotokan, Mitsusuke Harada arrived in England in November 1963, via Brazil, France and Belgium, becoming the first Japanese karate instructor to take up residence in Britain. Harada, although of the Shotokai (there was a split in Shotokan in Japan in 1957 as a result of Funakoshi's funeral, but this will not be gone into here) taught Shotokan. Harada had a truly wonderful lineage, having been a private student of both Gichin Funakoshi and Shigeru Egami. Harada had also been in the same class as the legendary Yoshitaka Funakoshi at the Shotokan *dojo* in Tokyo. Harada had actually taught for the BKF at its London *dojo* in November 1963. He had been brought over to England by judo legend, Kenshiro Abbe, and had formed the British Karate Council (and later, Karate-Do Shotokai). The two biographies[50,51] that chart his life, in detail, make no reference to any female students during the period in question. Further correspondence with Harada on this point has not produced results.

There were other instructors representing different styles who were also active to 1966, but whether they had or encouraged women students is unknown, though in Tatsuo Suzuki's Wado-ryu, we know that women did train, at least from 1966, but one may reasonably assume that karate was open to them in 1965. Bell, in a letter to Braine dated 3rd November 1966, noted that Suzuki's All Britain Karate-Do Association 'appears to be the largest, numerically, in Britain at this time' but that it was only formed the year before. However, one must also consider the newly formed KUGB, for they had two Japanese masters at the helm. Bell also wrote that: 'There are other organisations of karate in Britain, formed in the last year, all of which represent different systems of Japanese karate ...'

Robert Boulton, a 2nd Dan, had trained in Japan and was successfully teaching the Kyokushinkai karate of Matsutatsu Oyama, in London (at the London Karate Kai) and had been doing so for some time. Stephen Arneil, from Northern Rhodesia, as was, also of the Kyokushinkai, came to Britain in 1965 directly from Tokyo, where he had resided for some four years training under Oyama, and had graded to 3rd Dan. Boulton and Arneil then formed British Karate Kyokushinkai. In 1966, Arneil was graded to 4th Dan and was made manager and coach to the British All-Styles team.

The BKF's dominance of British karate, with its old, some might say affectionate, yet eccentric style of operation, had, after some eight years, finally come to an end. The writing was on the wall in 1964, unrest began to manifest itself in earnest in 1965, and competition grew at an extraordinary pace. With the appearance of more senior instructors and, in particular, resident full-time Japanese, Bell was eclipsed. Nevertheless, his place in the history of karate is assured, for he left an enduring legacy, and, as part of that, encouraged women to take up the art from the outset.

REFERENCES & NOTES

1. Layton, C. *Shotokan Dawn: A Selected, Early History of Shotokan Karate in Great Britain (1956-1966)*, Vols. I & II (Springlands Publishing, 2002; Mona Books, 2007).
2. Layton, C. *The Shotokan Dawn Supplement* (Mona Books, 2007).
3. Layton, C. *The Liverpool Red Triangle (1959-1966) & The Formation of the Karate Union of Great Britain* (in press).
4. Layton, C. *Shotokan Dawn Over Ireland: A Selected, Early History of Shotokan Karate in Eire (1960-1964)* (Aiki Pathways, 2006).
5. Layton, C. *Shotokan Dawn, Vol. I*, pp. 83-84.
6. Layton, C. *Shotokan Dawn, Vol. I*, p. 85.
7. Layton, C. *Shotokan Dawn, Vol. I*, p. 111.
8. Layton, C. *The Shotokan Dawn Supplement* (Mona Books, 2007), p. 35.
9. In an unknown newspaper, yet '*Recorder/Review*' is discernible.
10. These three reports would have come from newspapers from the Hornchurch area.
11. Layton, C. *Shotokan Dawn, Vol. I*, p. 111.
12. Layton, C. *Shotokan Dawn, Vol. I*, p. 67.
13. Layton, C. *Shotokan Dawn, Vol. I*, p. 112.
14. Layton, C. *Shotokan Horizon* (Mona Books, 2007) for a detailed account.
15. Layton, C. *Shotokan Dawn, Vol. I*, pp. 206-214.
16. Wingrove, T. Communication with C. Layton: 12th September 2006.
17. Layton, C. *Shotokan Dawn, Vol. II*.
18. Layton, C. Interview with Pauline Bindra: 2nd February 1994.
19. Layton, C. *Shotokan Dawn, Vol. I*, p. 244.
20. Seaton, W. Communication with C. Layton: 25th September 2006.
21. Layton, C. *Shotokan Dawn, Vol. I*, pp. 287-288.
22. Layton, C. *Shotokan Dawn, Vol. I*. p. 287 for a complete list.
23. Layton, C. *The Kanazawa Years: Reminiscences of Michael Randall, 7th Dan, on a golden age in British karate* (Shoto Publishing, 1998).
24. Layton, C. *Shotokan Dawn, Vol. I*, pp. 289-290.
25. Layton, C. *Shotokan Dawn, Vol. II*. p. 127.
26. Layton, C. *Shotokan Dawn, Vol. II*, p. 68.
27. Layton, C. *Shotokan Dawn, Vol. II*, pp. 69-70.
28. Layton, C. *Shotokan Dawn, Vol. II*, p. 105.
29. Layton, C. *Shotokan Dawn, Vol. II*. pp. 106-108 for a complete list.
30. Layton, C. *Shotokan Dawn, Vol. II*. p. 141 for a complete list.
31. Layton, C. *Shotokan Dawn, Vol. II*. p. 158 for a complete list.
32. Layton, C. *Shotokan Dawn, Vol. II*. p. 170 for a list.
33. Layton, C. *Shotokan Dawn, Vol. II*, p. 183.
34. Layton, C. *The Liverpool Red Triangle (1959-1966) & The Formation of the KUGB* (in press) for the other side of the argument.
35. Layton, C. *Shotokan Dawn, Vol. II*, pp. 161-162.

36. Layton, C. *Shotokan Dawn, Vol. II*, p. 186.
37. Layton, C. *Shotokan Dawn, Vol. II*, pp. 189-190.
38. Layton, C. *Shotokan Dawn, Vol. II*, p. 190.
39. Layton, C. *Shotokan Dawn, Vol. II*, p. 190.
40. *Daily Mirror* (25th October 1966), p. 25.
41. Layton, C. *The Shotokan Dawn Supplement* (Mona Books, 2007), p. 100.
42. Seaton, W. Communication with C. Layton: 28th September 2006.
43. Adamou, N. Communication with C. Layton: 13th September 2006.
44. Thompson, G. Communication with C. Layton: 26th September 2006.
45. Thompson, G. Communication with C. Layton: undated, but 2002.
46. Layton, C. *Shotokan Dawn, Vol. II*, p. 144.
47. Layton, C. *The Shotokan Dawn Supplement* (Mona Books, 2007), p. 106.
48. Layton, C. Interview with Dorothy Naylor: 28th December 2006.
49. Muthucumarana, D. Interview with Dorothy Naylor: 2nd January 2007.
50. Layton, C. *Karate Master: The Life and Times of Mitsusuke Harada* (Bushido, 1997).
51. Layton, C. *Reminiscences by Master Mitsusuke Harada* (KDS, 1999).

APPENDIX I

THE AGE OF FEMALE MEMBERS OF THE BKF AT THE TIME OF THEIR APPLICATIONS, BY DOJO

Dojo	Nō	Average	Youngest	Oldest	Years Covered
London/ Upminster	3	29.00	19	43	1961–1966
Dublin	2	17.50	16	19	1963
Middlesbrough	4	17.00	14	21	1963–1964
Blackpool	3	19.33	16	21	1964–1965
Manchester	2	22.50	22	23	1965
York	1	20.00	20	20	1965
Stoke B	1	29.00	29	29	1966
Bath	1	20.00	20	20	1966
BKF (all)	**17**	**21.29**	**14**	**43**	**1961–1966**
SD	**6.7**				
Including Naylor:					
Liverpool	1	32.00	32	32	1966
All	**18**	**21.89**	**14**	**43**	**1961–1966**

NOTES:
1. Bindra is included in the London *dojo* figures as the results are based on membership forms.

SD = standard deviation

APPENDIX II

FEMALE BKF STUDENTS (MEMBERS OR OTHERWISE) JULY 1957 – JULY 1966

Name	Applied to BKF	Dojo	Age/ Occupation	Comments
Higgins	1957 (no application form exists)	Hornchurch	Unknown	Special 6th kyu grading under Hoang Nam: 26th July 1957. Known only through references in a Bell/Plee letter
Doris Keane	1957 (no application form exists)	Hornchurch	about 17 Office worker	No BKF gradings recorded. Known only through one photograph & Bell's recollection
Suzette Hubbard	31st September 1961	London/Upminster (presumed)	43 Guest house proprietor	Prior judo experience (yellow belt) No BKF gradings recorded
Name unknown	1961/62 (no application form exists)	RAF Scampton (maybe a visitor)	unknown	Judo *gi* worn No BKF gradings recorded
Bernadette Berigan	8th August 1963	Dublin	19 machinist	Prior judo experience (blue belt) No gradings recorded
Carmel Bryne	24th September 1963	Dublin	16 shop assistant	Prior Judo experience No BKF gradings recorded
Pauline Bindra (née Fuller) (née Laville)	2nd March 1964 but trained prior to this	Middlesbrough/ London	19 typist	4 years prior judo experience (blue belt) some prior karate experience 8th kyu: 04/7/64[1] 6th kyu: 28/7/65[2] 5th kyu: 8/11/65[3] 4th kyu: 23/2/66[3] 3rd kyu: 20/4/66[4]
3 unknown	*1963/1964*	*Middlesbrough*	*Probably trainee nurses*	*Known from quotes from Bindra and Seaton*
1 unknown	*1964*	*London*	*unknown*	*Known from a quote from Bindra*
Denise Bedford	27th December 1963	Middlesbrough	16 coil winder	Prior Judo experience No BKF gradings recorded
Doreen Would	18th February 1964	Middlesbrough	21 upholsteress	Prior Judo experience No BKF gradings recorded

78

APPENDICES

APPENDIX II – *continued*

Name	Applied to BKF	Dojo	Age/ Occupation	Comments
Carol Tombs	21st May 1964	Middlesbrough	14 schoolgirl	Prior Judo experience No BKF gradings recorded
Doreen Draper	17th June 1964	Blackpool	21 alteration hand	Prior Judo experience 8th kyu: 04/7/64[1] Attended Lilleshall course. 6th kyu: 24/6/65[2] 5th kyu: 9/11/65[5] 4th kyu: 10/2/66[5]
Janet Revill	17th June 1964	Blackpool	16 shop assistant	No prior Judo experience 8th kyu: 04/7/64[1]
Rosemary Maine	25th June 1964	Middlesbrough	17 schoolgirl	No prior Judo experience No BKF gradings recorded
Carol Banks	4th March 1965	Manchester	23 housewife	No prior Judo experience No BKF gradings recorded
Margaret Abbot	5th March 1965	Manchester	22 aero dynamicist	No prior Judo experience No BKF gradings recorded
Wendy Varley	9th June 1965	Blackpool	21 typist	No prior Judo experience No BKF gradings recorded. Attended Lilleshall course
Mary McLaren	27th August 1965	York[6]	20 housewife	No BKF gradings recorded Later graded to at least 6th kyu KUGB
Suzanne Black	19th February 1966	London	25 chemist's assistant	No BKF gradings recorded
Joan Shaw	12th April 1966	Stoke B	29 housewife	No BKF gradings recorded
Janet Brannen	7th July 1966	Bath	20 wages clerk	No BKF gradings recorded
Dorothy Naylor (née Pemberton)	March 1966 Liverpool were members of the BKF until the end of March 1966, but did not register Naylor, or any other new members, at this time	Liverpool	32 housewife	KUGB gradings 9th kyu: 12/07/66 8th kyu: 12/07/66 7th kyu: 18/10/66
3 unknown but two first names known: Marilyn & Sheila	*March 1966*	*Liverpool*	*unknown*	*Known from a quote from Naylor, who recalled that Marilyn graded* 9th kyu: 12/07/66 8th kyu: 12/07/66

NOTES:

1. Bindra, Draper and Revill's 8th *kyu* were under Bell.
2. Bindra and Draper's 6th *kyus* were temporary under Kanazawa.
3. Bindra's 5th and 4th *kyu* were under Kanazawa.
4. The date given for Bindra's 3rd *kyu* may be 21st April 1966. She applied to grade at this time, but whether a grading actually took place for *kyu* grades, and if so, whether she was successful, is unknown. The entry is presented in the belief that she passed.
5. Draper's 5th *kyu* was under Kanazawa, her 4th *kyu* under Enoeda.
6. Nurses Almond, McDonald and Ashby began training in 1966 when the KUGB was formed and are not included on that basis. Whether the women merely practised self-defence as distinct from full Shotokan is unknown, as is whether they joined the KUGB.

No information about judo is given for Higgins, Keane, Black, Shaw and Brannen, through lack of data.

GLOSSARY

Age-uke – rising block
Aikidoka – student of aikido
Choku-zuki – straight punch
Chudan – middle level (chest height)
Chudan (soto) ude-uke – middle level outside forearm block
Chudan yoko-geri-kekomi – middle level side thrust kick
Dan – (the higher the dan, the higher the rank)
Dojo – training hall (literally, place of the Way)
Gedan-gamae – lower level guard (*gedan barai*)
Gi – practice suit
Gohon-kumite – five-step sparring
Gyaku-zuki – reverse punch
Hanmi – (hips) half facing (45°)
Heian – peaceful mind (a Shotokan kata)
Heian Nidan – 2nd Heian kata
Heian Sandan – 3rd Heian kata
Heian Shodan – 1st Heian kata
Heian Yondan – 4th Heian kata
Jiyu-ippon – one-step semi-free (sparring)
Jodan – upper level (head height)
Jodan empi – upper level elbow (strike)
Judoka – student of judo
Karateka – student of karate
Kata – forms (set movements in set sequences)
Kiba-dachi – straddle-leg stance
Kihon ippon-kumite – basic one-step sparring
Kokutsu-dachi – back stance
Kumite – sparring
Kyu – non black belt grade (the lower the kyu, the higher the rank).
Mae-geri – front kick
Mawashi-geri – roundhouse-kick
Nukite – spear-hand
Oi-zuki – lunge punch
Ren-geri – consecutive kicking
Sanbon-renzuki – three consecutive punches
Sensei – teacher
Shodan – 1st Dan (lowest level of black belt grade)
Shotokan – a style of karate (literally 'hall of Shoto')
Shuto – knife-hand
Shuto-uke – knife-hand block
Teisho-uchi – palm-heel strike
Ude-uke – outside (forearm) block
Ushiro-mawashi-geri – back roundhouse-kick
Yoko-geri-keage – side snap-kick
Yoko-geri-kekomi – side thrust-kick
Zenkutsu-dachi – front stance

INDEX OF SURNAMES

ABOUT THE AUTHORS

Clive Layton was born in Hertfordshire in 1952, the son of an architect. He began his martial arts training with judo in 1960 under Terry Wingrove, and started Shotokan karate in 1973 under Michael Randall and the Adamou brothers, Nick and Chris, gaining his black belt from Hirokazu Kanazawa in 1977. Originally studying environmental design, he later read for M.A and Ph.D degrees from the University of London, and is a Chartered Psychologist, Chartered Scientist and teacher. Doctor Layton has appeared on both BBC television and radio in connection with his academic work. A prolific writer, with one hundred publications, including twenty-one books on karate and numerous learned research notes, he has emerged not only as probably the most productive, but, arguably, the finest writer on Shotokan in the world. He has co-authored with famed Okinawan Goju-ryu master, Morio Higaonna; former British manager/coach to the world champion All-Styles karate team, Kyokushinkai master, Steve Arneil; the founder of British karate, Vernon Bell; Michael Randall; and, fellow historian, Harry Cook, amongst others. Doctor Layton's biography, *Kanazawa, 10th Dan*, and, *Funakoshi on Okinawa*, a portrait of life on Okinawa in the 19th century, have been published to much acclaim, as has his two volume work, *Shotokan Dawn*, which charts the first ten years of Shotokan karate in Great Britain, and, *Shotokan Dawn Over Ireland*, which provides an account of the formation of Shotokan in Eire, from 1960–1964. He has also acted for many years as a consultant reader to the journals, *Perceptual and Motor Skills*, and, *Psychological Reports*, on experimentation into the martial arts. Any spare time is taken up researching new books, pursuing his love of archaeology, genealogy and film, and enjoying the peace of rural life, by the sea, with his wife, daughter and labrador. A highly innovative and deep-thinking *karateka*, he currently holds the rank of 7th Dan.

Dinushni Muthucumarana was born in 1972, the daughter of a teacher and orthopaedic surgeon. An army cadet at school, she later joined Guys and St.Thomas' Hospitals, London, where she was first exposed to the martial arts. She later became a member of the Harrow *dojo* of *Sensei* Nick Adamou, from whom she received her Shotokan black belt in 2005.

Dr. Muthucumarana is a Fellow of the Royal College of Ophthalmologists and has published articles in the journal, *EYE*, the GP magazine, and in *BMA News* (published by the British Medical Association). She enjoys gardening, listening to music and spending time with her husband (a Shotokan 3rd Dan) and two children.